ORR

G J Sandusky *Latest Ed.*

HARVARD UNIVERSITY MONOGRAPHS
IN MEDICINE AND PUBLIC HEALTH

Editorial Committee

Walter B. Cannon
A. Baird Hastings
James Howard Means
S. Burt Wolbach

Executive Secretary
Katherine R. Drinker

LONDON : HUMPHREY MILFORD
OXFORD UNIVERSITY PRESS

BORDERLANDS OF PSYCHIATRY

BY

STANLEY COBB

Bullard Professor of Neuropathology
Harvard Medical School

Psychiatrist in Chief
Massachusetts General Hospital

CAMBRIDGE, MASSACHUSETTS
HARVARD UNIVERSITY PRESS
1944

COPYRIGHT, 1943
BY THE PRESIDENT AND FELLOWS OF HARVARD COLLEGE

SECOND PRINTING

PRINTED AT THE HARVARD UNIVERSITY PRINTING OFFICE
CAMBRIDGE, MASSACHUSETTS, U.S.A.

To
L. S. C.
"Of loyal nature and of noble mind"

CONTENTS

INTRODUCTION		ix
I.	BODY AND MIND	3
II.	THE PARALLEL EVOLUTION OF SPEECH, VISION AND INTELLECT	23
III.	SPEECH AND LANGUAGE DEFECTS	36
IV.	THE FUNCTION OF THE FRONTAL AREAS OF THE HUMAN BRAIN	54
V.	THE ANATOMICAL BASIS OF THE EMOTIONS	72
VI.	CONSCIOUSNESS	90
VII.	CONCERNING FITS	103
VIII.	PSYCHONEUROSIS	116
IX.	PSYCHOSOMATICS	149

INTRODUCTION

THIS IS NEITHER a textbook nor a monograph; probably it is best described as a series of essays on a group of subjects that have long been of especial interest to the author. These subjects have often been neglected because they were neither orthodox medicine, nor psychiatry, nor neurology. They have fallen between three stools. Therefore, when in the autumn of 1940 I was asked to give a series of lectures for the Lowell Institute, I gladly took the opportunity to discuss these subjects in a brief way. The book does not follow the lectures closely, but is an elaboration with a more medical orientation and much new material.

The subjects treated are collected under the title "Borderlands of Psychiatry" not because they are unimportant, but because historically psychiatry was for so many years confined to the study and treatment of the "legally insane." Thus many psychiatric problems in the community were not recognized or were left to irregular practitioners. Only recently has the psychiatrist come out of the State Hospital to take up the treatment of disorders of speech, emotion, and consciousness. The great problem in psychiatry will probably always be the "committed hospital patients," represented by the inner circles of Figures 1A and B. No less important, though less urgent, are the problems in the borderland that are too often overlooked. Here are found at the present time in the United States (see outer circle, Fig. 1B) approximately six and a half million partially incapacitated persons.

The 600,000 hospital inmates are divided into segments representing various percentages of the whole, according to diagnosis. Schizophrenia with 49 per cent is seen to be the greatest menace to mental health; in fact, because of its preva-

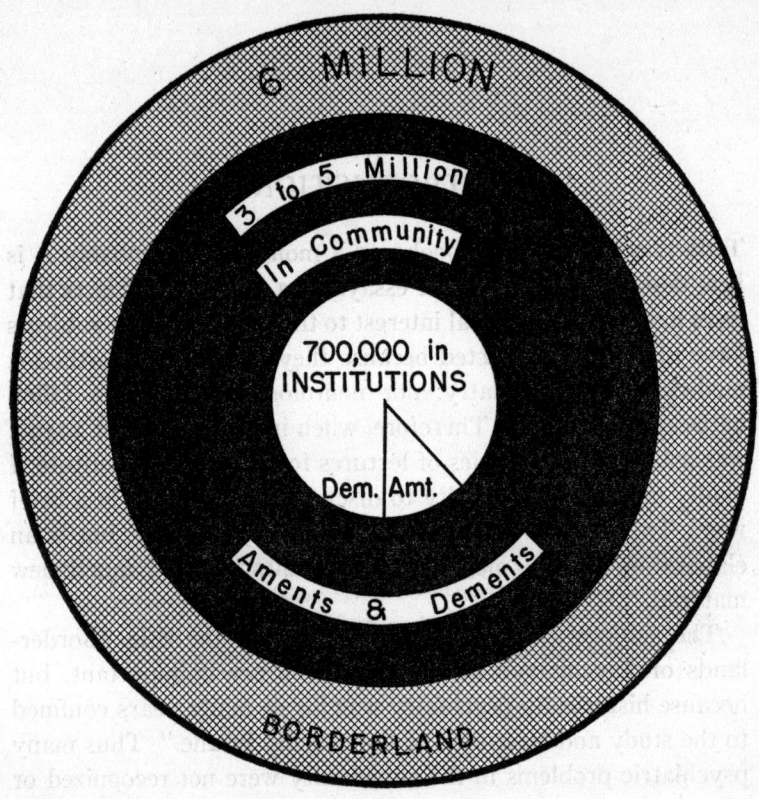

FIG. 1A

The problem of psychiatry in the United States in 1943 is diagrammatically indicated by the concentric rings. The inner ring represents the 700,000 mentally disordered patients in institutions. About 100,000 of them are "aments" (Amt.), i.e., they are lacking in mind and always have been; they are mentally defective or feeble minded. The other 600,000 are mentally diseased, they have "dementia" (Dem.) of one sort or another (see Fig. 1B); they have more or less lost their minds.

The middle circle represents the aments and dements in the community. The estimate of 2,500,000 mentally defective persons (aments) is probably fairly accurate. The remainder (600,000 to 2,500,000) is a very rough estimate of the number of persons with mental disease, living in the community, who could be legally committed to a mental hospital if necessary. The lower figure is taken from the opinion of those who say "There are at least as many psychotic persons outside of the mental hospitals as within their walls." The high figure is computed from the admission and discharge rates of mental hospitals, which show that thousands of patients wait many months before admission and others are discharged while still demented but harmless. (See Dayton (1) and Elkind (2).

The outer circle is the "Borderland" about which this book is written. It is further elaborated in Figure 1B.

lence and chronicity, it fills more hospital beds than any other known disease. The other mental disorders are less overwhelming, but constitute a great burden upon society.

This inner circle is of course the central problem of psychiatry. The care and study of these patients is the professional occupation of a serious and devoted band of psychiatrists who man the medical staffs of the mental hospitals of the country. These physicians and the body of medical and psychological knowledge which they represent are the basis of psychiatry.

The outer circle, however, is larger because greater numbers of people are involved, although most of them are less seriously ill. It is this area that I call the borderland, and like most frontiers it is often either disputed or despised territory. Neurologists, general medical practitioners, and even non-medical therapists of various types claim much of it. Certain areas are poorly defined — like the problem of speech defect, often called psychiatric by the neurologist, and neurological by the psychiatrist, and now being explored by the non-medical clinical psychologists and pedagogues. Stammering is a great problem, as is indicated by the estimated number of 1,200,000 stammerers, but there are also a great many patients with aphasia and other defects of speech resulting from neurological lesions. These are included in the segment called "other neurological." The number given here, 500,000, is the least satisfactory of the estimates — in fact, it is little more than a guess based on the rate of admission of neurological as compared to general medical cases in large hospitals. The number is probably considerably larger because of the fact that neurological disorders are notably chronic. Epilepsy is another borderland, claimed and disclaimed by neurologists, psychiatrists, and internists. Fairly reliable information has been gained as to its incidence in the general population by the rejections for this cause in draft armies and by such investigators as Lennox (3). Psychoneurosis is a most difficult field to define and measure. If one takes as his definition of neurotic a patient who seeks medical advice for relief of

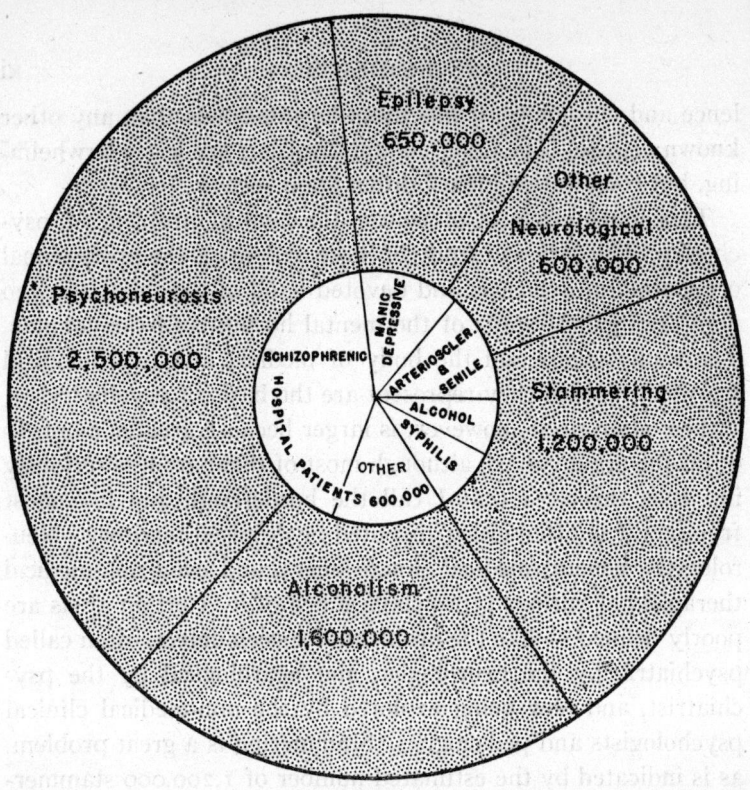

FIG. 1B

Diagram to give a more detailed idea of the borderland and central circle shown in Figure 1A. For some of the figures given there is good evidence; for others, the estimate is little better than a good guess. For the central psychiatric group (inner circle) the 600,000 patients, excluding feebleminded in mental hospital, fairly exact data are obtainable. The division into schizophrenia, 49%; manic-depressive, 10%; arteriosclerotic and senile, 9%; alcoholic, 5%; and syphilitic, 4%; is adapted from Dayton's figures for Massachusetts. As for the outer circle — the borderland of psychiatry — there are a number of good surveys (3) that indicate the amount of epilepsy in the community. The incidence of severe stammering is well known from many school and college surveys to be a little less than 1%. The estimate of the number of "alcoholics" is taken from Haggard and Jellinek (6), but it depends so much on definition that great variation is to be expected in the figures of different investigators. The incidence of psychoneurosis is extremely difficult to discover; two surveys (4) (5), however, come so close to the same figure that it is used as an approximation when "psychoneurosis" means a personality disorder severe enough to cause the patient to seek medical help or be advised to seek help. Milder degrees of maladjustment are almost universal. The least dependable figure on the chart is the 600,000 "other neurological" patients; these are the patients living on with damaged central nervous systems from various causes. The estimate is a guess made from the number of neurological and neurosurgical admissions to general hospitals. "Psychopathic personality" is not given a separate division; some of these fall under psychoneurosis and some under "neurological" because of cerebral trauma.

a disorder largely due to environmental maladjustment, then some sort of a figure can be gained by using Sydenstricker's (4) survey of Maryland where he found 11 psychoneurotic patients per 1,000 of population. This is well backed by Lemkau in a smaller urban district, who estimates that something over two per cent of the population present personality disorders that need attention (5). If all emotional maladjustments are counted, then "all the world is queer but thee and me, and thee's a little queer." Anyway the estimate of 2,500,000 is doubtless far too small even for those medically treated. Alcoholism is not taken up in a special chapter because I have no special experience in the field, but it most certainly must be included as one of the borderlands of psychiatry. The men who "can neither get along with liquor nor get along without it" form a great legion of misfits and potential inmates of mental hospitals. Every sort of physician tries to help them, with or without the aid of ministers, psychologists and reformed drunkards. A conservative estimate of the number of men and women today in the United States who are definitely injured by alcoholic intoxication is 1,600,000 (6).

The sexual perversions are not given a separate heading because most of them can probably be classed as neurotic. There are some homosexuals, however, whose trouble is at least partly due to endocrine disorder. Psychopathic personality is another diagnosis I have not put in the schema. This is not because it is unimportant, but because the more of these strange misfits I see, the more I believe that some of them have an encephalopathy. The others probably suffer from "psychoneurosis"; as a subdivision one might call them "character neuroses."

REFERENCES

1. DAYTON, N. A.: Mental disorders, statistical summary of admissions, discharges and deaths. Commonwealth of Massachusetts, 1939.
2. ELKIND, H. B.: Psychiatric Quarterly. 13:165. 1939.
3. LENNOX, W. F.: Science and seizures. Harper & Bros.: New York, 1941. 258 p.

4. SYDENSTRICKER, E.: Study of illness in a general population group. Pub. Health Reports. 41:2069–2088. 1926.
5. LEMKAU, P., TIETZE, C., COOPER, M.: Report of progress in developing mental hygiene component of city health district. *Am. J. Psychiat.* 97:805–811. 1941.
6. HAGGARD, H., JELLINEK, E. M.: Alcohol explored. Doubleday, Doran & Co.: New York, 1942.

BORDERLANDS OF PSYCHIATRY

CHAPTER I

BODY AND MIND
(*Psychosomatics*)

> For this is the great error of our day in the treatment of the human body, that physicians separate the soul from the body.
> PLATO, *Dialogues*, circ. 380 B.C.

> The concept of psychophysiological unity is the basis of enlightened monistic philosophy and is the only concept which agrees with and is supported by the laws of nature.
> AUSTEN FOX RIGGS, *Medical Record* 73:1071, 1908.

CASE I

A WOMAN of twenty-five entered the Massachusetts General Hospital in September 1934 because of painful, ulcerated finger tips. She looked worn and older than her years but still retained a certain youthful attractiveness of manner. She was from a fishing village in Rhode Island where her Portuguese parents had brought her up in a decaying Yankee culture. Considering her race, she had always been a reserved child and kept her sorrows to herself. Her mother died when she was twelve, and she immediately took over responsibility for her three younger brothers. Two years later her father remarried, and this she seemed to accept as inevitable. At the age of seventeen she married a man several years her senior; in spite of squabbles they had a good relationship and much happiness. At the end of a year a son was born, and for the next two years things went along reasonably well. Then she learned that her husband had been already married, that the former wife was alive, and that her marriage was illegal. The shock was great, but she decided to stick by her husband. They planned to separate for a year, during which he would get a divorce from his wife and then legally marry our patient. During the year of separation he visited her too frequently, and impregnated her, and the plans for divorce and remarriage failed. He went to California; she tried to produce an abortion by taking ergot but failed, and then married a local fisherman, much older than herself, because she needed a home and protection. Shortly after this marriage the second son was born and rather gracefully accepted by the new husband. Three years later she became pregnant by her second husband. The record reads:

Mrs. B's first attack of Raynaud's disease occurred under the following circumstances. She was and had been for some time carrying on a correspondence with her first husband who was in California. Her second husband had forbidden the continuance of this correspondence but she kept it up despite him. On a hot summer day of 1933 she had gone to the post office expecting to find there a letter from her first husband. When she asked for the mail, the clerk said that her husband had already called and taken it. This meant to her that her second husband had therefore found the letter; she believed that he would have recognized it, opened and read it, and she feared the consequences. She knew that he would resent the tone in which her first husband wrote to her. Badly frightened and trembling, she went out into the street. There she formed the plan of drowning herself and the two boys (by her first husband). At this same time in which she was trembling, fearful, forming ideas of suicide, she noted suddenly that the little finger of her right hand was numb and white, while the fingernail was blue. She was so struck by this change in the condition of her little finger that she went into a grocery store and showed it to an acquaintance. This condition continued for about an hour until the patient returned home and immersed the finger in warm water.

Her second attack of Raynaud's disease occurred on the ensuing day: her husband revealed to her that he did, indeed, have the intercepted letter. She demanded that he give it to her; he refused; they had a scene. Then she went to the dock with her two sons, intending to drown herself and them, with the intention, that is, of carrying out the suicidal plan that had occurred to her in the street outside the post office. As she stood on the dock with her two boys she noticed that the fingers of both her hands had become blue and painful. Then a man appeared on the dock to prevent her carrying out the suicidal plan upon which she had been intent. She again attempted abortion

CASE I

NAME: The Lady Who Blanched
HEREDITY: Parents Portuguese
SIBLINGS: Three Brothers

HOSPITAL # 61 R.D.
DATE: 1937

YEAR	MEDICAL DATA	ILLNESS	SOCIAL DATA	AGE
1910			Born in Rhode Island	0
1911				1
1912				2
1913				3
1914	Tonsillectomy	▬▬▬		4
1915	Enuresis	▬▬▬	"High strung"	5
1916		▬▬▬		6
1917	Measles	▬▬▬	School	7
1918				8
1919			Reserved child	9
1920				10
1921				11
1922	Menses		Mother died; Family responsibility	12
1923			High school, bright	13
1924			Father remarried	14
1925				15
1926				16
1927			Married older man	17
1928			Son born; marital squabbles	18
1929			Separation from husband	19
1930	Headache	▬▬▬	Attempted abortion; married fisherman	20
1931		▬▬▬	Son born	21
1932		▬▬▬	Correspondence with first husband	22
1933	White fingers; Repeated arterial spasm	▬▬▬	Letter episode; plan for suicide	23
1934	Operations, r. & l.			24
1935				25
1936				26
1937				27

Fig. 2

by taking a medicine that probably contained ergot, but failed and went through with the pregnancy.

Since the sudden onset the patient has had such attacks almost daily with increase in severity. During the first year of her disease, the finger tips were affected, but recently the disturbance has extended to the mid-palm of both hands, and simultaneously has involved both feet, which become white and cold, but do not ache as the hands do. Accompanying these attacks, the patient felt her heart begin to beat faster and forcibly until she could feel it beating in her neck, and she feels dull pain over her heart. Immersion in hot water relieves the painful extremities, but turns them blue for about five minutes. The affected extremities have become puffy, her feet swell, and she has had increasing difficulty closing her fists so that she can now only close them half way. Small ulcerations have appeared on the finger tips. The attacks occur when she is cold, tired, hungry or scared.

Operations were performed in 1933 and early 1934, first on the vasomotor nerves of the left hand and then on the right. The ulcerations healed as the circulation improved and the attacks of arterial spasm ceased. She was referred to one of the hospital psychiatrists for psychotherapy.

Case II

Another case is that of the youth who was "griped." This is his own word, arising spontaneously, a part of that vigorous but only partly conscious type of language that imitates such visceral expressions as "disgusted" (bad taste), "I'll sweat it out of him," "It broke my heart," "He has no guts for it." Modern medicine is beginning to show that these phrases are literal expressions of biological facts. They are emotional expressions but are accurate physiologically and are not metaphoric. This boy, in fact, did not "have the guts" to stand up to his mother.

Born in Connecticut of Methodist parents, he was raised in a small Massachusetts city. The family consisted of a kindly father, congenial with the boy, a domineering mother on whom

CASE II

NAME: A Youth Who Was "Griped"
HEREDITY: Immigrant, Methodist Parents
SIBLINGS: Younger Sister

HOSPITAL # 12 M.C.
DATE: 1936

YEAR	MEDICAL DATA	ILLNESS	SOCIAL DATA	AGE
1914			Born in Connecticut	0
1915				1
1916			Moved to Massachusetts	2
1917			Sister born	3
1918	Diptheria	▬▬▬		4
1919				5
1920			Dependent on mother	6
1921	"Pneumonia"	▬▬▬		7
1922			Mother strict and domineering	8
1923	Hernia	▬▬▬		9
1924				10
1925	Emotional and tense	▬▬▬		11
1926		▬▬▬	Congenial with father	12
1927				13
1928		▬▬▬	High school	14
1929				15
1930				16
1931				17
1932			Graduates Engaged to Protestant girl	18
1933			Business school Work as welder	19
1934				20
1935			Breaks engagement	21
1936	Constipation Cramps and mucous	▬▬▬	Mother scolds; patient "griped" Engaged to Catholic girl	22
"	Atropine and advice Short attack	▬▬▬	Automobile accident and law suit	"
1937	Well		Married	23

Fig. 3

the boy was very dependent during his childhood, and a younger sister. The medical history reveals little except that the boy was "high strung" at the age of eleven. School years were successful and at graduation he started "keeping company with" a Protestant girl whom his mother knew and liked. This went on for three years while he learned a trade and held his first job. At the age of twenty-one he realized that he really cared little for the girl and broke off the engagement. The mother was irate, and scolded him endlessly, and the patient reports that this "griped him like hell." He revolted, went with a new crowd, and became engaged to a Catholic girl. During these months he first noticed constipation; later he began to have abdominal cramps and frequent bowel movements with mucous. Because of these symptoms he came to the Out Patient Department of the Massachusetts General Hospital, where he was treated by Drs. Jones and White (1). Therapy consisted of atropine, to relax the spasm of the intestinal smooth muscle, and discussion to make him understand his psychological impasse. The parents were also interviewed. Symptoms ceased, the girl was accepted by the parents and the boy has only had one recurrence of the mucous colitis, a short attack after an automobile accident that led to a lawsuit.

The life chart (Fig. 3) clearly shows the temporal relationship between the social and medical facts. Why this boy was affected in the gastrointestinal tract rather than the heart, the genito-urinary system, or the skin, is not known. That problem is further discussed in Chapter VIII, but the "psychosomatic" problem can be simplified down to the brusque statements that *the boy had nerve enough to oppose a domineering mother but didn't have the guts to see it through without medical help.*

Case III

The third case shows less of the direct physiology of the emotions; it is more a tragic sequence of events leading to inevitable disintegration by rather obvious ways. This young woman was brought to the hospital at the age of twenty-six because of weak, painful legs that would scarcely support her to walk across the room, sore mouth, skin eruption, delusions of persecution, and failure of memory. She was treated for several months as a bed patient, given massive doses of vitamins, and discharged improved to be watched in the Out Patient Department, with the diagnosis of pellagra. This seems a common enough medical problem. The cause of the disease does not appear, however, until the social history is added and correlated with the medical (see Fig. 4).

Annie was born in 1910 of Irish immigrant parents. She was the second of nine children. In her eleventh year the family had to move from their pleasant home in Worcester to a poor suburb; the father was beginning to drink noticeably, and social agencies had to help. Annie did poorly in school and left junior high school at fifteen to help at home. She took a job as a salesgirl in a small shop at sixteen and at eighteen married the son of a neighbor, a youth slightly her senior, with a steady laboring job. When the first child was born the next year the mother was a robust young woman weighing 136 pounds. The child, however, had a spinal malformation (meningocele) and died after a few weeks. Two healthy children were born in the next two years, and in 1932 she had a miscarriage. She was then twenty-two, tired, losing her teeth, and struggling to keep the home running. The husband began drinking; by 1934 his drunkenness was a difficult problem; she would have to go out at night, look for him in the saloons and bring him home. For this she needed courage, and she got it by taking a drink before she went out. Gradually she drank more, the house became slovenly, meals were irregular and badly cooked. Finally she became pregnant again, her weight had dropped to 103 when the child was born, and the house became so filthy that it was reported to the Society for Prevention of Cruelty to Children, who came in, took the children, and sent the mother to the Massachusetts General Hospital. After six months of treatment

CASE III

NAME: The Woman Who Drank in Self-defense
HEREDITY: Parents Were Immigrant Irish
SIBLINGS: Second of Nine

HOSPITAL # 28837

DATE: July 7, 1941

YEAR	MEDICAL DATA	ILLNESS	SOCIAL DATA	AGE
1910			Born in Worcester	0
1912				2
1914				4
1916			School	6
1918	Measles			8
1919			Not bright in school	9
1920	Mumps		Moved to suburbs	10
1921	Whooping cough		Poor neighborhood	11
1922				12
1923	Menses		Father drinks heavily	13
1924			Junior high school	14
1925			Leaves school	15
1926			Works in store	16
1927				17
1928			Married	18
1929	Weight 136		Child born and dies	19
1930			Child born	20
1931			Child born	21
1932	Carious teeth		Miscarriage	22
1933			Husband drinking more	23
1934	Begins drinking		Brings husband home drunk	24
1935	Very poor diet		Child born. Home filthy. S.P.C.C.	25
1936	Weight 103. Pellagra M.G.H. Neuritis Psychosis		Broken home	26
1937	Poor diet		Home reunited; not drinking	27
1938	Miscarriage. D.and C.op Slight neuritis		Mother died	28
1939	Weight 127. Better		Husband gets better job	29
1940	Well		Husband has regular job	30

FIG. 4

(as described above) and six months of convalescence the family were reunited and things went fairly well until another pregnancy started; she lost weight and showed renewed signs of neuritis. She was sent to the hospital, where a miscarriage occurred and she underwent a gynecological operation. Social agencies once more gave aid, and by early 1939 the patient was back with her children; she weighed 127 pounds and her husband had a better job. In 1940 she reported at the Out Patient Department for follow-up; she was found to have no symptoms of deficiency disease. She said her husband had a regular job and was not drinking.

Such a record not only brings out the importance of modern social work in diagnosis and treatment, but indicates that medicine and sociology are inseparable; in fact, in a broad sense, medicine is a subdivision of sociology.

Case IV

The fourth case is described to illustrate how catastrophic these psychosomatic illnesses may be. It is an example of a rare but well recognized disease of young women — *anorexia nervosa*, emotional loss of appetite; the adjective *maligna* might well be added, because the disease often ends in death. The psychological and social factors are remarkably similar in the different cases reported, and there is good evidence that these factors lead to a starvation of the endocrine glands and a general cachexia so profound that return to normal function is impossible even after eating is resumed. The typical picture is that of a girl of sixteen or seventeen who has a fat, aggressive mother; the problems of late adolescence are difficult, and the girl becomes disgusted with everything connected with sex. She strives to stay slim and boyish by dieting; the mother scolds and forces food on her. She seeks escape by excessive extraversion in work and play, eats less, loses weight, is disgusted by food, stops menstruating, and finally is hospitalized because she becomes too weak to carry on. Improvement by forced feeding is rapid, she returns home and repeats the same behavior until radical social readjustment or death puts a stop to the vicious cycle.

The case presented was not thoroughly studied psychologically, but presents the main points found in these patients (Fig. 5).

Rita was born in Boston of Armenian immigrant parents. She was in the middle of a large family, the oldest of which was a fussy boy who tried to help the mother in managing the children. The father was a decent but rather crushed person; the mother was the mainspring from which energy and decision flowed. There is little known about the patient's childhood, except that she was always constipated and was bright at school. The older brother picked her out as his favorite and kept pushing her ahead, telling her how much ability she had and arousing her ambition. The mother abetted this by expecting high grades and urging her to do extra work. She was too studious and seclusive to have many friends, but at sixteen began to have an obvious "crush" on a robust and somewhat older schoolmate. This girl put on weight rapidly and took to eating sweets in excess, and Rita was disgusted. The two girls made a pact to reduce weight by dieting, although Rita weighed only 118. She graduated from high school and was given money by the brother for a special stenography course, putting her ahead of her older sisters. Finishing this training, she tried for a job that her brother recommended; she missed it and both he and she were much "shamed" by the failure. Nevertheless she kept on studying, then found a job, took up dancing a great deal, and had a young man who began to pay some steady attention. The older brother did not approve of their activities and told her he was ashamed to be seen with her because she was getting so thin. About this time her menses stopped, and she did not have to think about dieting because she lost her appetite. Her excessively active life went on. When she was nineteen one of her older and more placid sisters took her boy friend away from

CASE IV

NAME: A Girl Who Was Disgusted **HOSPITAL #** 348566
HEREDITY: Immigrant Armenian Parents
SIBLINGS: Fourth of Seven **DATE:** 1935

YEAR	MEDICAL DATA	ILLNESS	SOCIAL DATA	AGE
1916			Born in Boston	0
1917				1
1918			Sister born	2
1919				3
1920			Sister born	4
1921				5
1922			Brother born	6
1923			School	7
1924			Brother born	8
1925				9
1926				10
1927				11
1928				12
1929				13
1930			High school. Bright	14
1931			Pushed by mother and brother	15
1932	Begins diet wt. 118		Crush on fat girl, disgusted	16
1933	Amenorrhea, anorexia		Graduates. Stenog. course. Misses job.	17
1934	Asthenia and dizzy		Over-active; dances	18
1935	Tonsillectomy		Sister steals beaux	19
1935	June, wt. Weaker 71 Discharged		Still on the go. M.G.H. O.P.D. referred mental hospital	
	Readmitted with "cold" Died wt. 63			

Fig. 5

her. She began to feel tired and had to push herself. Dizzy spells took her to the doctor, who advised tonsillectomy, which was performed in May. She weighed only 71 pounds and was advised to take a long convalescence but insisted on getting up and going out, took up dancing again, and was reported as "still on the go." At last her skinny appearance and spells of weakness frightened her mother, who had been endlessly scolding her and talking about food. The brother and mother brought her to the Massachusetts General Hospital, where she was put to bed, persuasively fed on the medical ward, and discharged to the Out Patient in September, somewhat improved, with the diagnosis of "anorexia nervosa." This brought her to the Psychiatric Clinic, where the gravity of the situation was brought to the attention of the mother and brother. They refused to send the patient to a mental hospital, although she was "on the go" again and they were much alarmed. In November they brought her in to the emergency ward. She was exhausted, weak, weighed only 63 pounds, and had a respiratory infection like the mild influenza then prevalent. She was admitted to the medical ward, developed a diffuse pneumonia, and died in three days. Autopsy showed cachexia, atrophied ovaries, small adrenals, and a normal pituitary. The pneumonia was the immediate cause of death.

Case V [1]

The last case report is that of a twenty-one-year-old girl from a backward community in Maine. Her father was alcoholic and her mother was feeble-minded. At six months of age she had whooping cough and at eighteen months she fell into a cesspool and was nearly drowned; the immersion caused pneumonia, and "for six weeks she lay between life and death." At six she

---

[1] For a more detailed account of this patient, see the report by M. E. Cohen and S. Cobb on "The Use of Hypnosis in the Study of the Acid-base Balance of the Blood in a Patient with Hysterical Hyperventilation." *Res. Pub. Assoc. Res. in Nerv. and Ment. Dis.* 19:318. 1939.

had measles and reported them as terrible; frequent "colds" and otitis interrupted her school years. Nailbiting and sleepwalking are the first neurotic symptoms reported, but the whole history is that of an introverted child who made the most of every symptom and dramatized each illness.

After falling on her knee, "she went on crutches for a whole summer," and "had electric treatment for about a year." She also "kept throwing her back and hip out." At the age of twelve, there was an incident during which the patient alleged she was raped. More falls, a dog bite, a burn, and fainting spells further incapacitated her, and eventually she gave up school.

Tonsillectomy, appendectomy, German measles, trouble in her ears, legs, and knees, and a long period on crutches followed her leaving school (see Fig. 6). She left home to do housework with long hours and for low wages. Then she began to twitch. She says, "I don't know how it came on, I was twitching all over. I had a fever, was unable to eat or sleep much. My right side got so I couldn't move it. My face drew down on that side. My eyes went blind and I was unable to see for about three or four weeks." A physician diagnosed this as Sydenham's chorea and put the patient to bed. An osteopath told her to get out of bed and the twitching became better. Finally our patient, who had taken to religion, was cured of this twitching by divine healing. Her description of the healing is as follows: "It was a wonderful experience. I didn't believe much in it. My friends teased and teased me to go. Ten or fifteen gathered around me and I sat in a chair; they anointed me with oil and the minister laid his hand on my forehead. They all prayed; he prayed, and they all prayed afterward; I prayed also. I was lost in prayer; I didn't know whether people were there or not. I was lost in prayer talking to God. I could see him plainly as I can see you. He has long, wavy hair and a curly mustache and whiskers. He isn't beautiful or handsome, but he is beautiful. He seemed to have his hand on my head, seemed as if when I walked forward he walked with me, with his hand guiding, and then it was as if

CASE V

NAME: The Girl Who Panted **HOSPITAL #** 352919
HEREDITY: Alcoholic Father, Feeble Minded Mother
SIBLINGS: Third of Six **DATE:** 1938

YEAR	MEDICAL DATA	ILLNESS	SOCIAL DATA	AGE
1915			Born in Maine	0
1916	Convulsions Pneumonia		Fell in cesspool	1
1917	Mumps		Brother born	2
1918				3
1919	Chickenpox			4
1920				5
1921	Measles			6
1922	Otitis Nail biting		Began school	7
1923				8
1924	Fractured arm. Sleep walking and talking.		Brother born	9
1925				10
1926	Menarche Strangling feelings			11
1927	Minor injury to knee Crutches for 3 months		Story of rape incident	12
1928	Menstrual cramps		Seventh grade	13
1929	Knee and crutches again			14
1930	Tonsillectomy Arm bandaged		Falling off at school	15
1931	Fainting spell		Scared by drunken father	16
1932	Vomiting "Nervous breakdown"		Father died Stopped school. Earns $4 a week	17
1933	"Kicked by a child" and on crutches		Another rape story. Earns $5 a week	18
1934	Fainting, blindness, paralysis		Caring for sick grandmother	19
1935	Headaches Choreic movements		Brother married Divine healing	20
1936	"Tetany" "Chorea"		Caring for asthmatic patient M.G.H.	21
1937	Improved		Discharged, back at work	22
1938	Hospital for tetany		Working again	23

FIG. 6

he drifted out of sight. I seemed to shake all over for a minute, and there I was standing in front of the people and I didn't twitch after that."

The patient remained in comparatively good health until she began keeping house for a woman with asthma. Coincident with one of her mistress's severe attacks, the patient started to have spells of "panting for breath." She said: "My hands got numb and clenched up; also my feet started to turn in at the ankles." The attacks were rare at first, but gradually increased in frequency until she had one every day. The patient continued to breathe rapidly, her hands remained closed, and she was sent to Dr. J. C. Aub, who made the diagnosis of tetany and hysteria and referred her to the Psychiatric Clinic of the Massachusetts General Hospital.

Physical examination showed panting respiration at the rate of 140 per minute. She appeared little disturbed, although her hands were clenched and her feet extended and inverted. When asked the chief complaint, she said, "My ears," indicating that she had had otitis for many years. Her indifference to her situation was in marked contrast to the severity of her symptoms. Mental status showed special preoccupation with religious ideas, haziness as to exact dates and sequences of events. Information was poor and intelligence low. There was complete lack of insight.

During the patient's first day in the hospital, attempts were made to stop the carpal spasm by having her breathe into a bag or hold her breath. The responses were quite variable. She was later hypnotized several times, and it was always possible to restore her breathing to a normal rate and rhythm by suggestion. By post-hypnotic suggestion the breathing remained normal for an hour or more after hypnosis. The effect gradually grew longer until the patient was finally free of hyperventilation.

During the hypnotic treatments it was noticed that the position of the clenched fists was due to a combination of hysteria and tetany; there was an hysterical dramatization of the tetanic carpal spasm. In one experiment it was shown that while the patient's blood still showed alkalosis the hypnotic suggestion: "Open your hands!" caused the patient to unclench her fists, but the hands immediately took the typical position of carpal spasm. Then the suggestion: "Breathe slowly!" caused the respiratory rate to return to normal and the hands relaxed. In other words, by hypnosis it was possible to differentiate and remove the signs of hysteria which overlay the signs of tetany, and finally to remove the tetany.

The observations on this patient are unique because it was possible to study a case of hyperventilation tetany by chemical analysis of the blood and then, at the same sitting, after curing the tetany by hypnosis, to study other samples of blood and show that they were normal. Moreover, the chemical changes in the patient's blood were extreme (2), and illustrate that grave, demonstrable chemical changes can be wrought by the hysterical process. Conversely it was proved that "objectively demonstrable changes" in the patient's blood chemistry were produced by hypnotic suggestion.

Take any one of these case histories and try to draw the line between "mental and physical" ("psychic and somatic," "functional and organic"). Any one of these pairs of adjectives that try to cut the world in two then becomes equally futile. In the first case bigamy, guilt, fear, and suicidal fantasies were followed by arterial spasm in the hands and necrosis of the finger tips. In the second case a tense, dependent boy became resentful towards his mother who was directing his love affairs and during his struggle for emancipation suffered from mucous colitis. Case number three is a long story of slums, pregnancies, fatigue, and sorrow leading to alcohol, deficient diet, and pellagra. The fourth case recounts how a girl became disgusted, dieted to stay boyish, permanently injured her endocrine glands, and died of inanition. The last case briefly reports how a girl was almost drowned, said she was twice raped, took to panting as an expression of fear, developed severe tetany, and was cured by suggestion. One may go through these histories and put one's emphasis on either side: the psychologist could reasonably state that the symptoms were caused by guilt, fear, resentment, sorrow, disgust, and fright; the physiologist could lay the symptoms to arterial spasm, intestinal contraction, vitamin deficiency, inanition, and alkalosis. In each case the pathologist could have described marked changes of the tissue: ulcer of the skin, exudate in the gut, dermatitis and stomatitis, muscular atrophy and blood pH of 7.61.

Each history is a sequence of human events affecting the social, psychological, physiological, and medical aspects of the patient's life. Even the surgeon and the undertaker are called in, but the geneticist and psychologist would seem to have good ideas as to what started the ball rolling down hill. In fact, I confidently challenge any believer in dichotomies to draw the line between "mental and physical," "functional and organic" manifestations in any of these cases. It cannot be done because there is no such line.

If the line were drawn by the orthodox pathologist it would separate those symptoms which were caused by lesions visible with or without the microscope from those caused by invisible disorders of matter. He would designate as "functional" the spasm of the arteries that he cannot see in his specimen and the alkalosis of the blood determined by the chemist, but tomorrow he would have to call them "organic" when he gets a better microscope or a new scope of some sort on which he can rely. In fact, the line drawn by such a pathologist will be purely artificial, depending on the technical equipment available to him in 1943. Likewise the physiologist and the psychologist can factually draw no lines, as is shown in Chapters VIII and IX.

I solve the "mind-body" problem, therefore, by stating that there is no such problem.[2] The dichotomy is an artefact; there

---

[2] There are, of course, plenty of problems concerning the "mind," and the

is no truth in it, and the discussion has no place in science in 1943. Metaphysicians can argue the problem *ad nauseum*, and their nausea will be the proof of their futility.³

Instead of the dichotomies I offer a simple classification of the phenomena based on observed facts and any university catalogue or hospital report. All disorders can be classified pragmatically under one or another of such headings as Psychological, Neurological, Dermatological, Medical, Surgical, Obstetrical, Social, etc. The disorders may be simple and be called symptoms, or if more complex, syndromes, or even full-fledged diseases. In any case the classification holds; it is not dependent upon abstract concepts; it is practical, and gives to the patient a label that guides him to the proper professor or proper department to look after his trouble.

The problem of causality in medicine is a difficult one. The cause of a disease may be glibly said to be a certain microorganism, for example, the tubercle bacillus. This is never true; the situation is more complex. At the simplest level there is always the matter of "the soil on which the seed falls," i.e., the state of the human body in which the tubercle bacillus finds itself. The body may be in "good condition" and resistant, or "run-down" and susceptible. Something is known of sensitiveness and immunity, but little is known of the life happenings that lead up to these conditions. In fact one has to return to a clinical study of the train of events that led up to the moment of examination. Besides knowing pathology and bacteriology, one must know about the *him* or *her* under study.

Satisfactory classification of disease, nevertheless, will always have to go back to causes, and one must do as well as possible with the facts at hand. Therefore in psychiatry I believe at

---

"body," and all intermediary levels of integration of the nervous system. What I wish to emphasize is that there is no problem of "mind" *versus* "body," no problem of *either* "mind" *or* "body," because biologically no such dichotomy can be made.

³ Those wishing more reading on this line can get it in the study of general semantics (4).

present that the best one can do is to reduce the multiplicity of probable causes to four [4] main categories: *genogenic* or hereditary, *histogenic* or due to visible lesion of the tissue, *chemogenic* or due to ultramicroscopical changes in structure, and *psychogenic* or due to maladjustments in interpersonal relations (3). Theoretically a disorder may be purely genogenic (or any of the other three); practically, disorders are almost invariably found to be of complex genesis. The symptoms of Case 5, for example, were obviously chemogenic (alkalosis) and psychogenic (hysteria), but the patient also had a low level of intelligence, which was genogenic, and the early pneumonia probably left some histogenic scars. It is a matter of relating all the pertinent facts and giving to them their proper clinical emphasis.

In summary, I would insist that the old dichotomies "functional or organic," "mental or physical" are not only wrong, but lead to bad habits of thinking because they lead to static and obsolete ideas and do not allow for modern pluralistic and dynamic ideas of matter and structure (4). Physiology is the basis of clinical diagnosis, and no physiologist would accept for a moment the clinical jargon that uses the word "functional" to denote "psychogenic." Anybody who stops to think realizes that no function is possible without an organ that is functioning and therefore no function takes place without structural change. Every symptom is *both* functional and organic. It is never a question of "either–or."

The difference between psychology and physiology is merely one of complexity. The simpler bodily processes are studied in physiological departments; the more complex ones that entail the highest levels of neural integration are studied in psychological departments. There is no biological significance to this division; it is simply an administrative affair, so that the university president will know what salary goes to which professor.

---

[4] There is nothing magic about four; five, ten, or twenty may be more true. I only insist on being pluralistic and practical.

This distinction between psychology and physiology will be discussed more fully in Chapter VIII.

REFERENCES

1. WHITE, B. V., COBB, S., JONES, C. M.: Mucous colitis. Psychosomatic Medicine Monograph I. 1939.
2. TALBOTT, J. H., COBB, S., COOMBS, F. S., COHEN, M. E., CONSOLAZIO, W. V.: Acid-base balance of the blood in a patient with hysterical hyperventilation. *Arch. Neurol. & Psychiat.* 39:973–987. 1938.
3. COBB, S.: Foundations of neuropsychiatry. Williams and Wilkins: Baltimore, 1941.
4. KORZYBSKI, A.: Science and sanity. Science Press: Lancaster, 2nd ed., 1942. 806 p.

CHAPTER II

THE PARALLEL EVOLUTION OF SPEECH, VISION AND INTELLECT

> Man verwechselt immerwährend die Begriffe der evolutiven Vererbung des Gehirns (und entsprechend der Seele) mit denjenigen des Kulturfortschrittes. Erstere braucht Jahrhunderttausende oder gar Jahrmillionen, um den Menschen wie alle hohern Tiere wesentlich zu ändern; letzterer dagegen ist eine reine Erwerbung im Laufe des Individuallebens.
> A. FOREL, *Der Weg zur Kultur*, 1924, p. 74.

THE brain is the organ of mind. Only professional quibblers doubt this. Of course the brain has many other and more lowly functions, such as keeping the organism alive by respiration, vasomotor control, and locomotion. Intellectual productions are, neurologically speaking, results of the functioning of the most highly organized neural mechanisms, which are in the most complex cortical level and represent the acme of integration. So the brain is the organ of paramount interest to psychologists — the true *sine qua non*. Important as other organs may be — eyes, ears, muscles, uterus, and gonads — they can have no psychic effect unless there is a functioning brain to bring them together, to add up the score and express the result. In short, to integrate everything that goes on in the body and give it meaning.

One of the simplest ways to gain an idea of the workings of this most complex of organs is to study comparative anatomy (1). Everyone has a rough idea of the behavior of such common animals as the rat, dog, and monkey. Even a superficial study of the brains of these animals, and a comparison of their brains and behavior patterns with those of man, leads to important conclusions. The lower or basal parts of the brain are much alike in all mammals. Here are the centers for vegetative life and automatic and reflex behavior. It is the higher levels that are of interest to the psychologist and student of comparative behavior. Thus the simple mapping out of the functions of the surface of the cerebrum is significant.

For example, taken in simple terms, the rat may be said to be a rodent that lives a largely nocturnal existence, relies on smell, touch, and hearing more than on vision, and has relatively simple motor habits. All four limbs are used almost entirely for locomotion and comparatively little for exploring and manipulating things. The rat is a keen animal, is adaptable even to man's rapid changes in culture, but is quite limited in learning capacity (2); his survival is due more to his keen senses than to his reasoning ability; he can solve only simple problems; but he feels extraordinarily quickly when to run away. A glance at the sketch of the rat's cerebral hemisphere (Fig. 7A) shows that tactile, auditory, and especially olfactory sense have large areas; vision is poorly represented, and only a small area is left blank as "unaccounted for."

The dog is an animal capable of learning much more complex tricks and of solving more difficult problems than the rat, yet his sensory behavior is not very different. He depends largely on smell and hearing; touch is less important, and vision is relatively undeveloped. The dog's motor functions are simple. The cerebral map (Fig 7B) shows this clearly. It is important to note that the cortex, or mantle of brain that lies over the lower centers, is larger in proportion to the brain stem (cf. Figs. 9 and 10) and that a deep sulcus has appeared between the frontal and temporal lobes; in fact this sulcus is the result of the expansion of the cortex backward and downward, making the temporal lobe. Also note that a considerable space in the cortex is left blank between the areas recognized as associated with the special functions designated as motor, tactile, visual, auditory, and olfactory.

The next step is a rather long one to the chimpanzee, a pri-

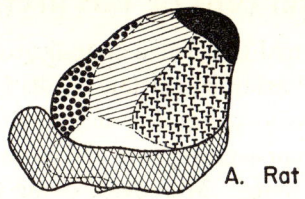

A. Rat

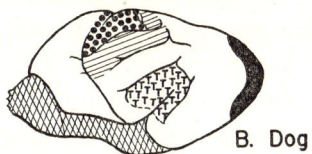

B. Dog

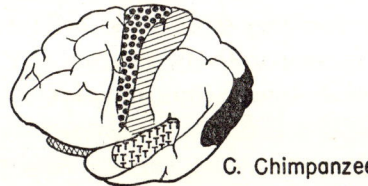

C. Chimpanzee

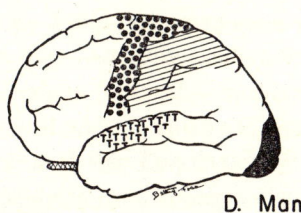

D. Man

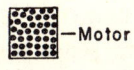 —Motor   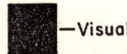 —Visual

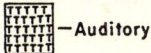 —Auditory   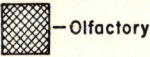 —Olfactory

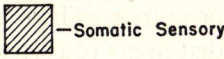 —Somatic Sensory

Fig. 7

mate. Here is an animal that has a complicated motor life; his combined ground and arboreal existence calls for individual use of all four limbs. His locomotion is not confined like the rat's and dog's to simple, four-legged paces and a few awkward movements of individual limbs. Moreover, living and traveling in trees calls for keen vision, hearing is less important, and smell is least used. Apes of this type can learn tricks and solve fairly complex problems, but they are not much superior to the best dogs in this respect.

The map of this monkey's brain (Fig. 7C) shows the great development of the cortex as a whole; the temporal lobe is definite and the deep fissure (of Sylvius) is longer than in the dog. The special areas for vision and tactile sense are much larger than in the dog. Auditory sense is less well represented, and the olfactory bulb is comparatively insignificant. The blank areas are somewhat more conspicuous, especially that in the frontal lobe.

Figure 7D represents the left cerebral hemisphere of a human brain (3), diagrammatically mapped out to correspond with the other three mammalian brains. The student is at once struck by the relatively enormous areas left blank and the rather small size of the special areas for auditory, visual and tactile sense, and for motor organization. Olfactory sense is so poorly represented that it is almost invisible in this lateral view. No one sensory area is greatly developed; all four are about equally represented in the cortex, smell largely on the hidden mesial surface.

And herein lies the superiority of man: in his development he did not specialize on any one or two sense organs, developing them to a high degree at the expense of the whole. All are developed evenly. Thus from one area to another there have developed association tracts, coördinating the senses, and the sensory areas with the motor output. These association tracts have become so important that areas of cortex have developed to subserve these elaborative and associative functions. Around each main receiving station (sensory area) is an area for elaboration of the crude sensory impression. The stimuli are spread and related to other sensory stimuli and to former impressions somehow stored in memory. In the sketches of dog and monkey brains these associative areas appear as blank areas somewhat less extensive than the specialized areas. In man the development has gone far over toward association, so that the greater part of the surface of the brain is taken up with these more complex processes. Being more complex, more highly integrated, they are considered psychological in function. So one finds even in the early maps of the cortex such designations as a "visuo-sensory" area bordered by a "visuo-psychic" (4).

This development of associative areas can logically be explained by the lack of domination by any one or two senses; by the evenness of development and balance of the different senses with the motor output. Each receiving station had to have its long circuits to each other receiving station; and all had to send long circuits to the motor areas where sensory impulses, after elaboration and association, are transformed into action through the motor tracts.

In the simplest sort of mechanistic explanation, it seems that a sensory stimulus is received in the appropriate cortical sensory area; it then spreads over many associative fibres to other neighboring areas, awaking old associations (memories) and arousing responses conditioned by past experience. Eventually this process of spread of stimulus (long-circuiting) is concentrated and the impulses are projected onto the motor areas, to be transformed into motor acts. In short, the crude sensory stimulus arrives in the cortex, is widely spread so that former experiences are aroused, and is finally expressed in motor behavior. The greater the long-circuiting (5) through association areas the greater is the conditioning of the response. Reactions are delayed and modified by past experience. The more one acts in the light of experience, the more intellectual is the response. The ability to "look ahead" and act "intelligently" is the great asset of man. No other animal can do this to any important extent. It is the great expansion of the long-circuiting (in the blank spaces on the charts) that makes man human.

There is, however, one respect in which man specializes. He had a *leading hemisphere* and this means a leading hand. The common arrangement is for the left hemisphere to be dominant, causing right handedness and usually correlated right "leggedness" and "eyedness." About 75 per cent of persons are right handed (6), the remaining 25 per cent are divided between those who are left handed and those who are mixed in their dominance or ambidextrous. No satisfactory explanation is available as to why right is common rather than left. Many fanciful ideas have been put forward from the theory that the left hemisphere has a better blood supply than the right, to the heliocentric theory that the right hand dominates because man originated north of the equator and, looking at the sun, was impressed with the fact that great things move towards the right! Thus right became the symbol of rectitude and dexterity and things on the left were sinister. It is an interesting observation that about 70 per cent of human foetuses lie in the uterus in the "left occiput posterior" position, i.e., facing to the right. No one has ever found out whether or not these become the right handed majority of babies. Probably the dominance of right handedness is due to chance in heredity. If the homozygous right-handers were dominant, and the left-handers were recessive, with the heterozygous individuals divided between apparent right-handers and the ambidextrous, the Mendelian ratio would at least approximate the observed numbers.

Whatever the cause may be, cerebral dominance is an observed fact of great theoretical importance to the evolution of man as a superior mammal with a highly developed brain capable of intellectual processes. Two other occurrences in development are of equally fundamental importance; they developed with cerebral dominance and together the three brought forth intelligence and speech; I refer to the liberation of the

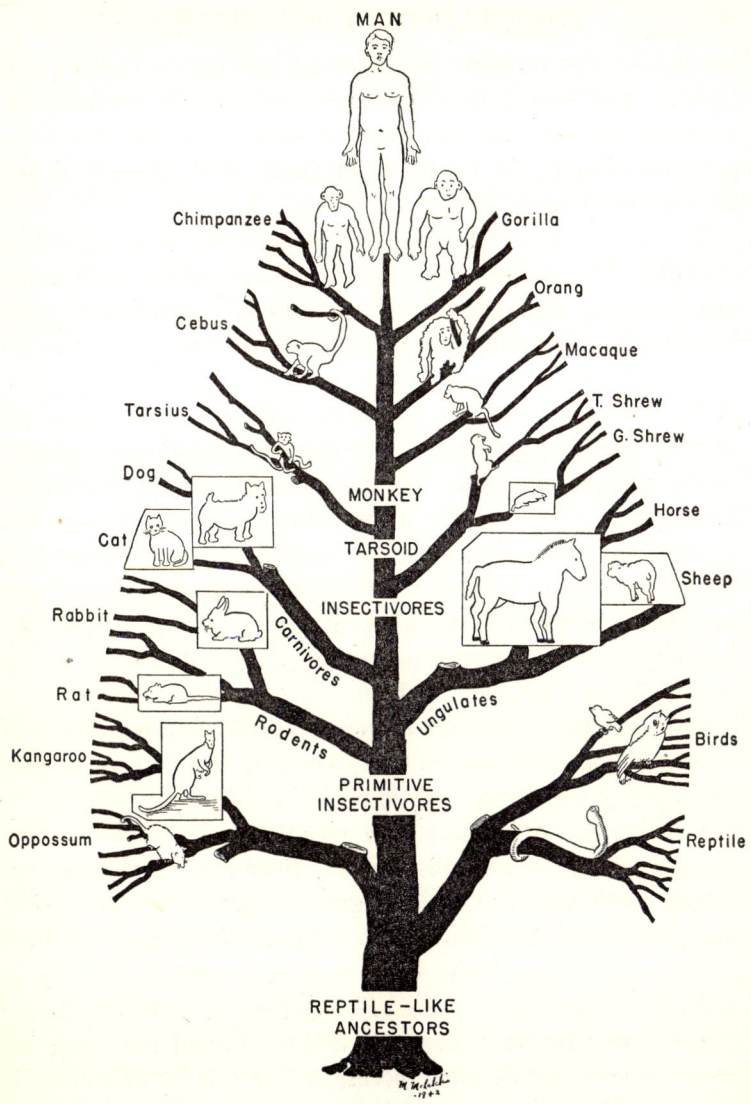

Fig. 8

Tree showing ascent of man from reptiles through insectivores (shrews) and monkey. This is the direct line. The animals that branch off have frequently attained high specialization, but none have reached any degree of intellectual accomplishment.

hands and the forward migration of the eyes. These made possible the coöperation of hands and eyes in exploration, accurate observation, and manual skill. This has been excellently brought out by G. Elliot Smith in his *Essays on the Descent of Man* (7).

To me it is easier to visualize the process as an ascent, a climbing of the family tree (Fig. 8). From our reptile-like ancestors to man there is a direct trunk-line of inheritance through the primitive insectivorous mammals to shrews, tarsius, monkeys, primates, and man. Other groups of animals (reptiles, birds, marsupials, rodents, ungulates, and carnivores) grew out as great specialized branches, becoming more and more specialized as they developed to the species now extant, represented as terminal branches on the chart. Each of these in his own specialty is superior to man: the rattlesnake can differentiate minute changes in heat, the bird has better eyes than man, the bat has better ears, the dog a better nose. But in each case man has the better combination because in his ascent he stuck to the trunk-line and did not branch off.

The insectivorous ancestors were adaptable to many diets and habitats. Some of them took to trees and here they developed tactile sense and motor skill in all four limbs to such an extent that they could sit up on a limb, free their fore-limbs from the routine job of locomotion, and use their arms and paws for skilled movements. Thus the ground shrew with its simple brain (Fig. 9A) lived largely in a world of smell as it poked about in the deep shade of grasses and shrubs. Taking to arboreal life, the tree shrew (Fig. 9B) shows a brain with increased areas for hearing, vision, and touch, and a decrease for smell. The environmental necessity for this development is obvious. The little tarsius (Fig. 10A) is one of the few remaining representatives of our tarsoid ancestors who improved on the tree shrew by further liberation of the forepaws to become hands, but especially by an extraordinary change in vision.

All primitive mammals and the majority of the higher forms

SPEECH, VISION AND INTELLECT

have eyes placed laterally in the head so as to make as wide a range of vision as possible. The combined visual fields of the two eyes encompass all of the horizon except that portion directly back of the occiput. This is an obvious advantage for

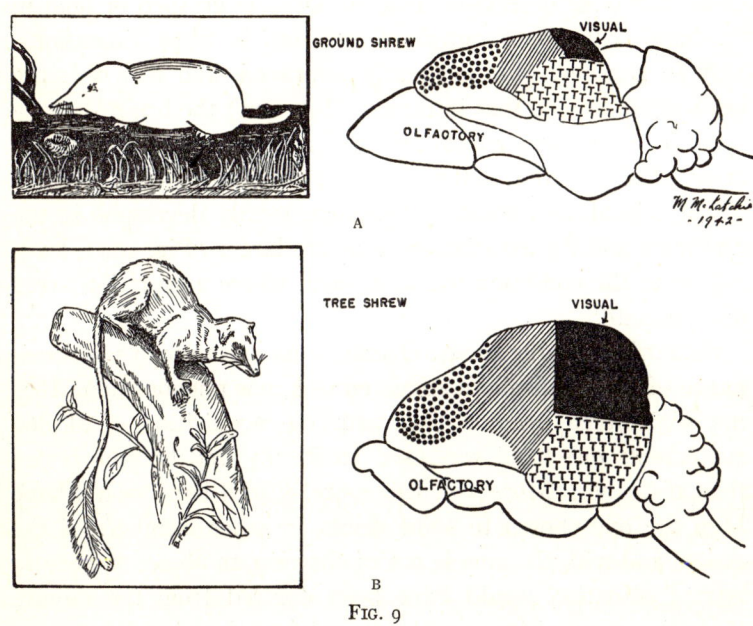

Fig. 9

The *Ground Shrew* has a primitive brain with very large olfactory bulb and relatively small cortical areas for motor function (dots), somatic sensory or tactile (parallel lines), visual (black) and auditory (TTT). The area left blank in the frontal region is very small.

The *Tree Shrew* is a more active animal with larger eyes, more anteriorly placed. Arboreal life calls for more complex locomotion, better vision and hearing, and less olfactory sense. The corresponding areas in the cortex show this.

(See G. Eliot Smith, *Essay on the Evolution of Man*.)

animals that are hunted, that depend on flight for safety. Aggressive hunting animals have eyes set more frontally so as to pursue more accurately and strike their prey. This is obvious below mammals in the hawks and owls. Carnivorous mammals such as tigers and wolves also show this adaptation, but the most highly developed stereoscopic vision is found in monkeys and man.

When the ground shrew climbed a tree and slowly evolved into a tarsoid, along with the freeing of his fore-limbs for use as hands, eyes became frontal, the fields overlapped, and binocular visualization of objects developed. Objects grasped or held in the hands could be scrutinized and seen in three dimensions. Skill in handling objects greatly improved, and with this the brain developed so that in tarsius (Fig. 10A) the brain shows a great increase in the visual area and a beginning of association areas. The evolution to the monkey stage is easy to understand: tactile, visual, and auditory areas are evenly developed in the cerebrum and the association areas are larger (Fig. 10B), leading on to the condition found in man, where association areas predominate.

Somewhere in the recent change from ape to man the dominance of one hemisphere appeared as a new phenomenon. It is not difficult to imagine that with the acquisition of skilled movements one hand was used habitually and became better than the other. Moreover, this more skillful hand would have been the one chosen to show things to other members of the group, and with the simple act of showing an object, sounds to attract attention would have been emitted from the mouth. Here began primitive speech, expletive at first but later combining with signs of the leading hand to symbolize something; with symbolization came language.

The leading hemisphere in the human cerebrum resembles the opposite subordinate hemisphere. No anatomical difference can be detected by present methods. In their function, however, they differ in this — symbolization is developed largely in the leading hemisphere. A tendency exists at birth for one or the other hemisphere to be dominant (the inherited aspect of handedness mentioned above), but if a leading hand is injured in infancy, skill will be acquired in the other hand. In short, the tendency is inherited, but each of the hemispheres has a poten-

SPEECH, VISION AND INTELLECT

tiality for development, and an infant forcibly made left handed, before speech develops, may become right brained.

Everything is represented in both hemispheres except the symbolic function. These are very largely (but probably not entirely) developed in the dominant hemisphere. Speech is not

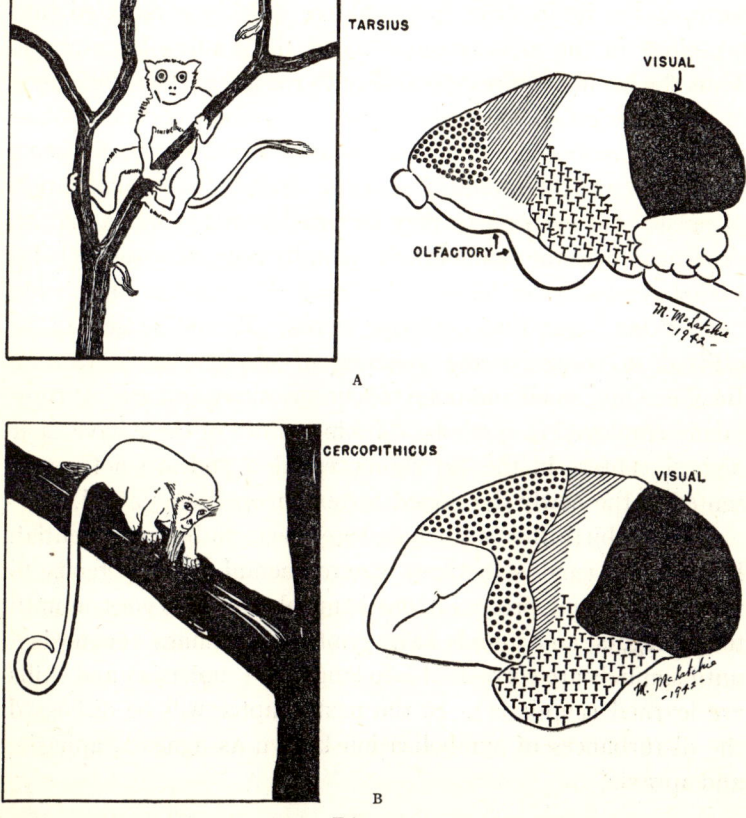

Fig. 10

In *Tarsius* the arboreal life has led to great locomotor skill. The eyes are very large and look directly forward. The olfactory lobe is less prominent, and the cortex as a whole is larger.

In a true *Monkey* (Cercopithicus) the olfactory bulb is hardly visible from a lateral view. The areas for motor skill, tactile, visual, and auditory sense are large and approximately equal. Blank frontal areas are conspicuous where *association* is presumably the chief function.

the only method of symbolization. All complex motor acts must be thought of and rehearsed mentally before they can be performed expeditiously. This is eupraxia, the learning of motor skills by symbolic thinking; it is essential for muscular education, especially manual dexterity.

Crude sense impressions arrive at the simple receiving platform of the brain (Fig. 7D) and are quickly elaborated into meanings in the association areas of the leading hemisphere. Thus the brain acquires the ability to recognize the significance of things, eugnosia. Sounds learned as symbols become spoken words; at more primitive levels sounds are understood not as words, but as expressions of emotion. Such is the symbolization of music; but even music may be written on a score so that an expert can read the symbols and mentally reproduce the melody. Visual symbols may be of many kinds, the most erudite being the written signs that compose words. Tactile sense can be utilized to recognize the meaning of objects, as in reading Braille. Only smell and taste remain primitive and are not commonly employed in symbolic thinking. Both of these have their highest centers in the old rhinencephalon and are not represented in the newly developed cortex (neopallium) at all.

Thus at birth the two hemispheres seem to be equipotential. Inheritance (and sometimes environmental injury) tends to start the learning process in one hemisphere. This goes on until touch, sights, and sounds have symbolic meanings (eugnosia), until symbols are correlated into language (euphasia) and skills are learned (eupraxia). In the next chapter will be discussed the disturbances of symbolization known as agnosia, aphasia, and apraxia.

REFERENCES

1. HERRICK, C. J.: Neurological foundations of animal behavior. Henry Holt & Co.: New York, 1924. 334 p.
2. LASHLEY, K. S.: Brain mechanisms and intelligence. University of Chicago Press: Chicago, 1929. 186 p.

3. BRODMANN, K.: Vergleichende lokalisationslehre der grosshirnrinde. Johann Ambrosius Barth: Leipzig, 1925. 324 p.
4. CAMPBELL, A. W.: Histologic studies on the localization of cerebral function. University Press: Cambridge, 1905. 360 p.
5. COBB, S.: Foundations of neuropsychiatry. Williams & Wilkins: Baltimore, 1941. 231 p.
6. WILE, I. S.: Handedness, right and left. Lothrop, Lee & Shepard Co.: Boston, 1934. 439 p.
7. SMITH, G. E.: Essays on the descent of man. Humphrey Milford: London, 1927. 195 p.

CHAPTER III

SPEECH AND LANGUAGE DEFECTS

> It seems but yesterday that the lamented Agassiz urged his pupils of Penikese Island to become "ambidextrous," if they wanted to become good naturalists; and my illustrious friend, Brown-Sequard, proclaimed at his Lowell Institute lectures "the equal training of both sides in our children as an urgent necessity."
> Dr. EDWARD C. SEGUIN (1843–1898), "Training Both Sides of the Brain," in *Hygiene of the Brain and Nerves and the Cure of Nervousness*, edited by M. L. Holbrook, M.D., 1878.

BEFORE attempting to enter upon the study of speech defects, the principles of long-circuiting, conditioning, balanced sensory development without specialization, and the appearance of a leading hemisphere in man must be thoroughly understood. They are described at some length in Chapter II. Without such a phylogenetic and neurological understanding of speech no one can adequately diagnose and treat speech disorders. Unfortunately, many speech specialists and trainers are narrow in their points of view and by riding hobbies confuse the field with one-sided theories. The schools run by non-medical teachers of speech are the most conspicuous in this regard. Their practice is often helpful, but their theory seldom bears thoughtful study. Even the physicians who have studied neurology and psychiatry vary widely in their theories as to causation of stammering: Orton (1) stands on the solid foundation of inheritance, physiology, and the theory of cerebral dominance (of which more later), while Sullivan (2) considers that stammerers have a special type of personality (an idea not borne out by my observations). Froeschels (3) has a developmental theory. Some psychoanalysts (4) think that stammerers suffer from "fixation of the pleasurable oral libido on speech" or from guilt feelings connected with early nursing pleasures. They would classify stammering as a "narcissistic neurosis." Robbins (5) considers that cerebral congestion causes the stammering.

In each of these theories there is probably some truth, but among those who specialize in speech training one rarely encounters the sound attitude that data must be gathered from all types of research in neurological, anatomical, genealogical, psychiatric, and psychological fields. Even the few workers who are thoroughly trained seem to be unable to weigh the evidence without bias. Many of them are prejudiced. The field is controversial, and no sound practice can emerge until the medical profession and the psychologists get together and do some significant investigation.

Like all important mechanisms of the nervous system, speech is represented at several levels. Fig. 11 shows diagrammatically six such levels of integration. These are discussed under headings named for the main symptoms recognized when each level is injured. Beginning with the simplest, the neuromuscular level, one proceeds upwards by way of the more complex cortico-bulbar and cerebellar levels to the cortex, where at least three levels of increasing complexity can be described.

1. Paralysis and Aphonia
(Neuromuscular level, Fig. 11, broken lines)

The neuromuscular neurons in Fig. 11 are shown as broken lines, arising in the nerve cells of the VII, X, and XII nuclei of the hindbrain and going outward to muscles of the lips, larynx, and tongue. This is the peripheral innervation of the organs of speech, and any interference therewith will cause obvious weakness of the muscles and functional loss. Since the lesions are usually along the nerve trunks they are likely to cause complete interference with the passage of nerve impulses. Thus the paralysis of the innervated muscles is complete even though often temporary. But the lesions rarely affect both sides, so the muscles on the normal side go on with their function and do a fairly good job. For example, the speech of a man with complete facial (VII) nerve paralysis on one side is somewhat blurred in enunciation, but perfectly understandable if the man makes an effort to speak distinctly. Likewise, paralysis of half

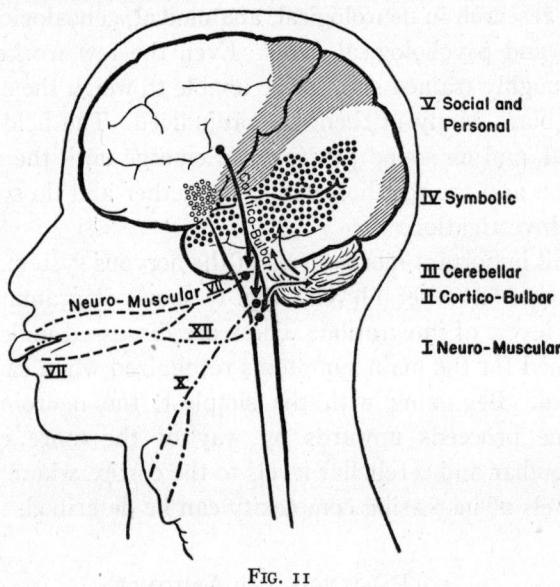

Fig. 11

Diagram of principal levels of speech integration (see text). The stippled area on the cortex shows the general localization of speech function; the part stippled with circles is the area for motor speed (Broca).

the tongue causes only slight speech difficulty. Bilateral paralysis of any of these muscles would of course cause marked loss of speech, even complete aphonia; words could not be articulated. The cause would be apparent because of the drooping and atrophied muscles. Lesions of the nuclei in the hind-brain (VII, X, and XII) can also cause paralysis of peripheral speech musculature with atrophy; this is rare, occurring as "bulbar paralysis" in progressive muscular atrophy and allied diseases.

2. Supranuclear or Pseudobulbar Paralysis with Dysarthria

(Cortico-bulbar level, Fig. 11, heavy line with arrows)

The great motor nerve cells in that part of cortical area 4 just above the Sylvian fissure send axons down to those nuclei in the medulla that control the peripheral organs of speech (vii, x, and xii). The tract consists of fibres projected from the cortical motor area to the nuclei of the peripheral speech mechanism. Interference with it, therefore, will disturb motor function, but not in the same way as at the neuromuscular level. In the first place no marked muscular atrophy will take place because the nuclei in the hind-brain are intact and the nerves to the muscles are functioning. It is only when this peripheral nerve mechanism is interrupted that conspicuous atrophy takes place. Secondly, each motor area sends motor fibres to nuclei in both sides of the brain stem (bulb), i.e., the innervation is bilateral so that interruption of one cortico-bulbar tract only will leave a good supply of fibres to both sets of nuclei, right and left. Unilateral lesion, therefore, at this level has little effect upon speech, causing, if anything, slight disturbances of articulation (dysarthria). If, however, there are scattered lesions in the brain and they happen to fall in both cortico-bulbar tracts, then, according to the severity of the lesions, there will be marked dysarthria or a speechlessness known as "pseudo-bulbar palsy." In this the tongue, lips, and larynx are paralyzed, the patient seems as incapacitated as in a true bulbar paralysis, but there is no evidence of injury to the neuromuscular level such as atrophy and muscular fibrillation. Moreover, the scattered cerebral lesions are likely to cause mental and emotional disturbances which locate the trouble at a supranuclear level. For example, outbursts of laughing and crying without accompanying appropriate emotion are likely to occur.

3. CEREBELLAR DISORDER WITH INCOÖRDINATION OF SPEECH
(Cerebellar level, Fig. 11, dark arrows from bulb to cerebellum to mid-brain and thalamus)

The cerebellum is the great motor coördinator of the nervous system. It has the function of making muscles work together for useful performance. When it (or any of its tracts) is injured, there is likely to be motor *disorder* — exactly that — the muscles work, but in a disorderly way. The symptom is called incoördination or asynergia.[1] This may affect arms, legs, or any part of the body. When it strikes the tracts that have to do with the organs and centers of speech, the effect is incoördination of speech, shown as lack of rhythm, monotony, explosiveness, staccato and scanning speech. The last is a sing-song expressionless way of talking best imitated by scanning Longfellow's "Evangeline." The abnormalities vary greatly in kind and degree, but they can be recognized by the fact that there is *disorder* of speech without evidence of paralysis or weakness.

CORTICAL LEVELS

When the brain stem is surpassed and the cortical levels are reached, it becomes evident that they can be variously described. Perhaps as meaningful a division as any is into cortical areas with the functions of (a) projection, (b) symbolization, and (c) association. The first are those areas that have long axons projected to or from brain stem and spinal levels. An example of this is the motor (cortico-bulbar) neuron already described. Other examples are the primary receiving stations in the cortex for visual and tactile stimuli. The simplest cortical mechanism for hearing, however, is probably in most persons already affected with meaning, i.e., there is a symbolic factor. The primary receiving station is in the medial geniculate body of the thalamus. Symbolization and its unilateral dominance and the special association areas will be described as follows:

[1] Lack of working together.

4. Cortical Disease with Agnosia, Aphasia, and Apraxia

(Symbolic cortical level — stippled areas, Fig. 11)

It is impossible to give an adequate description of this mechanism in a few pages, but a general outline may be attempted.

The senses important to language are vision and hearing (sense of touch replaces vision for blind people reading Braille, but it is secondary for normal people). The two main senses each have three levels of integration. Visual perception is localized in area 17 (Fig. 14), visual recognition in area 18, and revisualization in parts of area 19. A lesion at the first level causes *blindness*, at the second, loss of recognition (the patient does not know what the perceived object means, hence he has *visual agnosia*). A lesion in area 19 causes loss of power to revisualize scenes or persons. The patient cannot remember the plan of a house and cannot get home even though he may recognize the street or house he is seeing at the moment. He is *visually disoriented* because he cannot bring back a series of pictures.

The auditory sense has three cortical levels not so clearly defined as the analogous visual levels. The first cortical level, essential to primary perception, is the first transverse temporal gyrus of each side (area 41). Since the innervation is bilateral, removal of one such area does not materially affect the function of hearing; destruction of both produces cortical deafness. The second cortical level of hearing is a crescentic area of cortex on the lateral aspect of the temporal lobe (Wernicke's area) and is part of the superior temporal convolution. It is defined as the "paratransverse" area (41 and 42, Fig. 15). Destruction of Wernicke's area of the major side produces acoustic verbal agnosia; a similarly placed lesion of the minor side produces no recognizable symptoms. In acoustic verbal agnosia the patient may, for example, have lost his knowledge of the meaning of word symbols, but can still recognize a whistle, the sound of crumpling paper, etc., and say what is going on. Thus it is obvious that the acoustic mechanism is more concentrated in space in each temporal lobe (area 41), but has less unilaterality in the dominant hemisphere than is the case with the visual mechanism. The third cortical level extends backward and downward from Wernicke's area into the temporal lobe (areas 42, 21 and 22, Fig. 15) and is concerned with recall of auditory memories. Destruction of this area renders it difficult for the patient to reauditorize his words and consequently he cannot find them to express himself.

Recognition of learned symbols has been mentioned in respect to words heard; for words seen the center is in the angular gyrus, area 39, and a lesion here causes visual verbal agnosia, or "word blindness," as opposed to the "word deafness" resulting from a lesion in the temporal lobe.

So much for a brief description of the most important points concerning the receiving end of linguistic disorder, the "sensory aphasia" of older authors. The motor side is equally complex and depends on an understanding of the fact that no learned motor skill can be practiced without an ideational plan. This is a psychic elaboration necessary as a precursor to the carrying out of any complex motor act. This ideational planning is called eupraxia; the normal person knows how to do a thing quickly and almost automatically when requested. A defect of such performance in response to command is *apraxia*. It is a symptom of injury to the sensorimotor elaboration areas of the cortex, corresponding to agnosia from a lesion in the more strictly sensory area. In relation to most performances eupraxia is bilateral, the acts of one hand, for example, being planned in the opposite precentral and supramarginal gyri. Lesions of these areas (parts of 6 and 40) or their fiber connections may cause apraxia.

Apraxia of the organs of speech (tongue, lips, larynx) causes *motor aphasia*; the patient loses the memory of how to make the movements to articulate words; he may know just what he wants to say, but he cannot get the plan of the word into his mind. A lesion of Broca's area (44) causes this symptom. Much controversy once raged over "Broca's aphasia," but Nielsen's (6) summarizing of the data, including that from modern surgical procedures, leaves no doubt that motor aphasia has this precise localization. The cases that seemed to disprove it are probably cases in which area 44 of the minor side took over the function of motor speech readily; i.e., the patients were somewhat ambidextrous. Moreover, expletive speech is always possible with the minor side; only propositional speech is lost when the major area 44 is injured. In other words, the function of language is largely concentrated in the leading hemisphere, but a primitive sort of speech (emotional, expletive, habitual) is subserved in the homologous areas of the minor hemisphere. Areas 39, 44, 19, 18, and 17 are the most unilateral in function, areas 41 and 42 are less unilateral. Individual variation in relation to the degree of handedness is important.

Area 39 has the function of symbolic visual recognition, i.e., understanding letters and words by sight. Because words were first learned by hearing, however, area 39 cannot function if cut off from areas 41 and 42. During the process of learning to read, words are sounded out or told to one. Thus the portion of the temporal lobe lying between areas 39 and 42 is of great importance. This takes in the posterior part of area 22 and the upper part of area 37. A lesion here may cause as much loss of reading ability (alexia) as a lesion directly in area 39. Moreover, because language is learned by associating vision and hearing with objects and symbols, this area is particularly important. In fact, Nielsen (6) calls it "the language formation area."

Take, for example, the case of objective nouns, the simplest and commonest words used. They are names, usually of objects seen. So engrams must be stored in areas 22 and 37 correlating both visual and auditory meanings. That this is true is shown by cases of temporal lobectomy in which the language formation area of the leading hemisphere is removed. The result is *amnesic aphasia* or anomia. The patient has lost the storage mechanism for nouns; his "naming center" is gone. When shown a pen, he uses circumlocution and may reply "It's to write with" but cannot say "pen." *Anomia* is one of the commonest subdivisions of aphasia; it might be called the opposite of motor aphasia.

If one takes these main symptoms (which are well explained physiologically), agnosia, motor aphasia, and anomia, and adds the obvious complications, it is seen that many special sorts of aphasia are possible. But by sticking to the principles laid down, these strange phenomena can largely be explained and localized. For example, one can hear music as well as words; therefore "amusia" is found. One can learn several languages and have marked aphasia in one but little in another. Symbols used for mathematics are different from letters; so one may have agnosia for figures. In fact, loss of the ability to calculate is found after lesions in various areas and is not well understood. *Semantic aphasia*, a term coined by Head (7), should be mentioned because it is the commonest of all aphasias and is not localizable. It consists of a quantitative reduction in the capacity for and comprehension of speech. The victim has a little of all language functions left but cannot put sentences together or express any complex idea. This phenomena is present in persons with diffuse cerebral lesions commonly senile, in toxic patients, and in normal but excessively fatigued persons. In fact, almost all patients with aphasia have an element of the semantic form, and careful examination will usually show some mental loss. Semantic aphasia is a form of dementia.

Symbolization with its negative states of aphasia, apraxia, and agnosia makes a complex and difficult subject, yet it is a field capable of analysis by the neurologist. It is the borderland between physiology and psychology; claimed sometimes by both and at other times neglected by both.

5. Disorders of Cortical Dominance with Stammering and Reading Difficulty (Strephosymbolia)

(Symbolic level, stippled area, Fig. 11)

It is an old observation that reading and speech disorders are often associated with partial left handedness. Teachers and physicians owe much to Orton for his studies in this field, for clarification of the meaning of cerebral dominance, and for the practical relation of handedness to stammering and defects in reading and writing in children. Orton's (1) Salmon lectures and Wile's (8) book cover the field well. In Chapter II, I have described the evolutionary evidence for linking speech and binocular vision with a leading hemisphere. In man the fact is obvious, from a mass of clinico-pathological experience, that in a great majority of persons the left cerebral hemisphere is dominant over the right and these persons are right handed. The minority, perhaps 25 per cent, is made up of some left handed men whose right hemispheres are dominant, and more who are ambidextrous in various degrees and whose hemispheres have uncertain dominance. This uncertainty of dominance is much more common in infants than later in life when habit has settled the question. In other words a *tendency* to right or left handedness is inherited and is only consolidated into action by habitual use of one side as a leader. Evidence for this is found in children who inherit right handedness, but whose right hand is crippled by a birth palsy. They learn to use their left hands with perfectly satisfactory skill and some of them in making their motor shift to the right hemisphere carry the speech center to that side as well.

In spite of the fact that handedness is inherited, and therefore dependent upon the structure of the genes (genogenic, see page 21), no difference can be seen between the right and left hemispheres of the brain. Grossly and microscopically, nothing significant has ever been found to distinguish the dominant from the secondary hemisphere. The greater ease with which the left hemisphere takes over these functions is due to some ultra-microscopic arrangement of the matter that makes up the cortex. If the reader insists on classification (as of 1943) the difference is probably chemical rather than histological. To say that the trouble is "functional" is just as stupid in this connection as in others. There can be no function without a structure behind it, and function is not inheritable.

Orton has given a name — strephosymbolia — to this condition of uncertain cerebral dominance. Neither hemisphere takes the lead. When symbolization in speaking, reading, or writing is needed instantly there is delay and confusion because the leadership is mixed. Hesitant and stuttering speech results, and in reading and writing surprising bits of letter reversals in words reveal the relation of the trouble to handedness. For example a child will revert to his early impulse to read from right to left and read aloud "saw" for "was," "but" for "tub," etc. Clinical evidence was impressive that this mechanism of "mixed leads" caused speech and reading defects. Final proof, however, seems to have come from the laboratory, where Lindsley (9) made electroencephalograms of normal people and stammerers during speech. In normals the alpha rhythm of the brain waves was usually synchronous and smooth. In the stammerers the waves in the tracings from the two hemispheres were frequently out of phase and often obliterated, especially when blocking in speech was observed clinically.

It seems to me that "mixed lead" is an important cause of stammering and related symptoms in ambidextrous persons. Strong left handedness does not seem to predispose to speech and reading difficulty. Orton's methods of training, aimed at making the patient fix his lead in a chosen hemisphere, is an advance in therapy. One must not, however, think that every ambidextrous child will have difficulty in symbolization; perhaps 5 per cent of the population is somewhat ambidextrous and only about one per cent have speech difficulty. It is probable that ordinary childhood development takes care of most of the cases; habit and use cure the defect; the child "outgrows" his slight disorder. In the cases where the trouble becomes worse and lasts into adolescence and adult life, to become a real disability, one must look for additional causal factors.

From the standpoint of treatment, it would seem wise to let a left handed child work out his own salvation. Do not force him to be right handed in any way; the world will do that gradually because it is a right handed world the child is born into. The ambidextrous child needs more care; probably he will choose his lead at an early age and follow it, but if reading or speech difficulty develops, he will need visual, auditory, and proprioceptive training along Orton's lines to make one hemisphere (preferably the left) clearly dominant. The great desideratum is to accomplish the training with as little emotional stress as possible. Let it be simple and matter of fact. Rather than make it seem too important to the child, give it up, keep the home placid, and wait until the child wants help. Don't make him self-conscious about his speech defect by giving him elocution lessons or trick ways of getting the words out!

6. Psychoneurosis with Stammering

(Highest control level, area left blank in Fig. 11)

The function of speech is the most highly integrated of human functions; it follows that it is the most easily disturbed function. At all levels its smooth working may be interrupted and the clinical results are obvious, although too often overlooked as having medical significance. A description of the voice is rarely incorporated in a medical or even a psychiatric history, yet the examiner learns a great deal as soon as he listens to the patient's voice. He gets an "intuition" about the patient's "personality" during the interview, but he would be surprised if he analyzed this "intuition" into its components to find how much of it comes from his experience in life with different sorts of people with different sorts of voices. Everyone recognizes the fulsome boom of the self-satisfied egoist, the breathless, hasty voice of the struggling, ambition-ridden youth, the emotional tremolo and the strident staccato of the frustrated. The variations are legion, and only when hesitation becomes extreme or emotional blocking almost complete does the average clinician take note.

When put under unusual emotional stress, almost anyone stammers ("stutters" is a synonym). Arising to address an audience is enough to make many normal speakers stammer for a few moments, "until they get warmed up." Stammerers are people who habitually hesitate and stick in their speech under stress, but who can talk or read without hesitation when alone and relaxed. The trouble does not seem to be with the organs of speech, they often function well enough when the patient is alone with a sympathetic examiner; the essential trouble seems to be in the patient's social relations. He is "shy," cannot "put it over," is afraid to meet people, has varied anxieties, and especially has become fearful that he will stammer if called on to speak. Certain sounds are especially difficult, but these vary from month to month and year to year, so it is probable that *fear* of a certain letter is the cause of the sticking, rather than the sound formation itself. Any lead or bridge to start the speech and keep it going, like talking in unison or singing, will get rid of the stammer. Putting the patient on the spot by asking him a direct specific question will bring out the blocking in the speech.

For all these reasons stammering is thought to be a neurosis (see Chapter VIII) and there is no doubt of the importance of neurosis as a causative agent. Everybody probably has stammered at times. It is the child who *fears* that he will stick next time he tries to speak who perpetuates the stammering into an anxiety symptom that may last for months or years. Of course there are complicated neurotic mechanisms behind the fear about speech. The child is neurotically anxious and chooses speech as the symptom rather than vomiting, bed-wetting, food

SPEECH AND LANGUAGE DEFECTS 49

fussiness, or one of a host of other possible neurotic expressions. Why speech is chosen is not always obvious.

A carefully studied and long followed case is typical: Born in the middle of a large family, this boy was competitive with two older brothers. There was much emotional tension and fear surrounding the birth of a sister four years younger. About this time an episode occurred: three older children took the patient out in a gale of wind; they ran ahead of him and he was left alone; when he opened his mouth to call, the wind blew in and he was made speechless; the panic is still remembered forty-five years later. Some hesitancy in speech had been noticed before this but there was more afterwards. School was deferred until the age of eight. At that time speech was normal, but with reading aloud and school pressure stammering appeared again and was marked throughout six years of school and two years of tutoring. A stammering school helped only temporarily, because the patient soon learned that the "cure" depended on having faith in a trick way of getting started. Through college years the speech defect was bad. After marriage it improved, and work for one winter along psychoanalytic lines plus training in vowel sounds and reading aloud brought marked improvement. Family worries headed up four years later, and a relapse occurred. Then several months of Adlerian "individual psychology" (a sort of superficial psychoanalysis aimed at the patient's relation to family, job, and ambition in the reality situation) caused great improvement. Later a classical Freudian psychoanalysis helped some more. All of these improvements must be considered as aided by the general ageing process and settling down into a successful family and professional life.

The evidence in this case, especially the type of successful treatment, would seem to indicate that here was a case of stammering caused by fear and tension, perpetuated by anxiety; in short, this is a psychoneurosis. The patient, however, was later examined by Orton, who demonstrated ambidexterity. The family history was studied and is here shown (Fig. 12). Obvi-

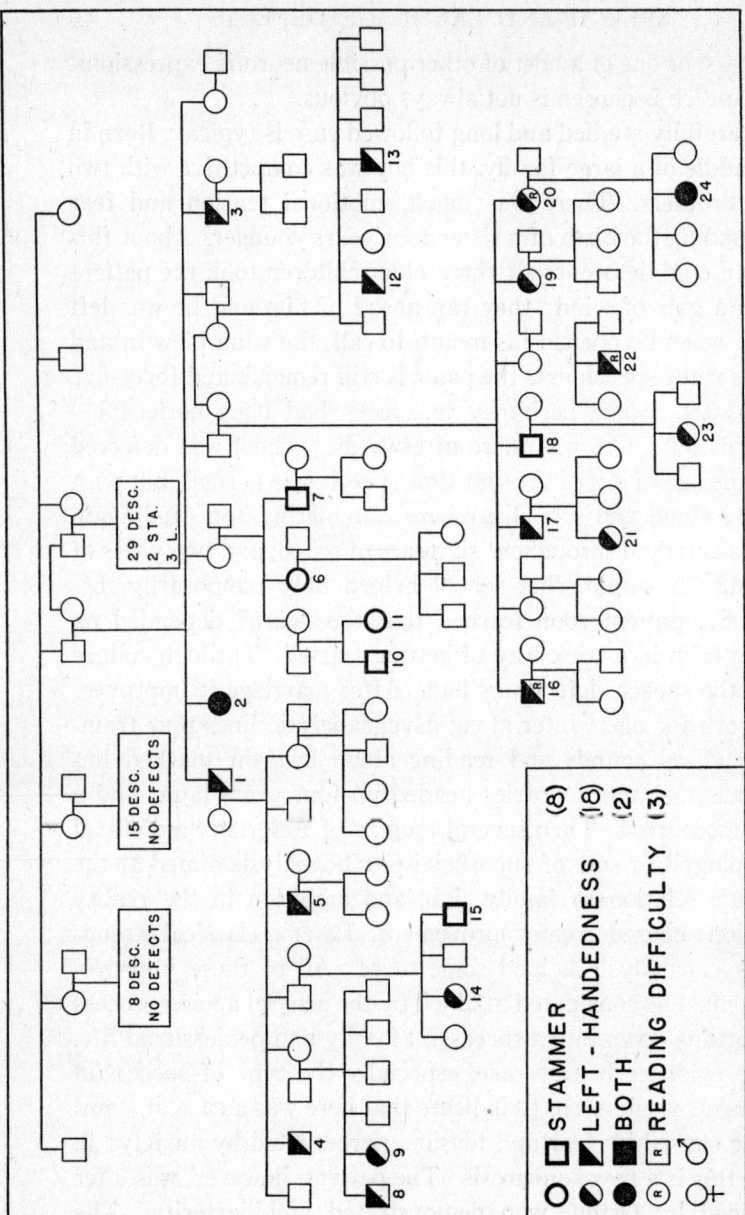

FIG. 12. Familial distribution of left-handedness, speech and reading defects in the case described. He is No. 18 on the chart; No. 2 had a rapid hesitant speech all her life with little real sticking; No. 4 is one of the 18 left-handers and has a marked lisp; No. 6 stammered in youth and has a residual hesitancy at 59; No. 7, No. 10 and No. 11 only stammered in childhood; No. 15 and No. 24 are still young. The reading defects known are No. 16, No. 20, and No. 22 — all were slow, laborious readers; No. 22 was greatly helped by treatment under Dr. Orton. Circles indicate females, and squares, males.

ously there was a large inherited factor in this man's stammering. Out of 77 persons in three generations there appear 9 speech defects, 3 reading defects, and 18 persons with left handedness. Only two of the left handers also stammered. Mild degrees of ambidexterity could not be found by this method of history taking, and some reading defects and cases of brief stammering were surely missed.

The lesson is the usual one in all studies as to causality — there is a multiplicity of causes. Not only did this boy inherit instability of his speech apparatus, but he was in a social situation where his interpersonal relations developed anxiety at an early age. The neurosis merely made use of the least resistant system and perpetuated the symptoms.

Localization of neurosis at any especial level in the central nervous system might be considered unjustifiable "neurologizing." But to carry out our schema in Fig. 11, it seems to me that one can say, without distorting the evidence, that the symbolic level is disturbed in this case by an inherited defect, probably in cerebral dominance. The psychoneurosis has to do with the patient's reaction to his environment, especially his interpersonal relations. The organ that subserves these functions is in all probability that part of the cortex that stores memories and makes associations and complex "conditioned reflexes." In other words no neurosis is possible without the association areas of the frontal, parietal, and temporal lobes.

Few cases of stammering have been carefully studied from the psychological standpoint. The statement by some psychoanalysts that it is an "oral neurosis" is backed by no good evidence, and seems to me to be somewhat naïve theorizing. Psychoanalysis has helped a few adult stammerers, but there are also failures. On the other hand some psychoanalysts have had a rather extensive experience in treating the episodes of stammering that occur in young children (10). Here the psychological factors are often immediate and obvious, and the children react to explanation with remarkable relief of symptoms. In these children the commonest cause seems to be a hurry and push of speech because of sibling rivalry, competition, and stress. Imitation of an older child or parent who stammers may start the symptom and anxiety may fix it. Cases are known where severe supervision of language, with strict prohibition as to what words may and may not be spoken, seems to be the etiology. The most dramatic group, however, are those where trauma to the mouth has precipitated an attack of stammering. One boy was gagged and left for hours in a cellar by playmates. Etherization and tonsillectomy are common precipitants of attacks. If that operation takes place at the age of two to five (when there is much wondering and fantasy about alimentation, mouth, bowels, urination and genitals) the terror aroused at operation may be translated into a general anxiety. The fears may spread to the problem of what else may have been cut out, and become connected with the universal question as to why girls and boys are not alike. One boy of four, for example, began stammering badly after he had seen the genitalia of a girl for the first time. A few weeks before he had undergone a traumatic experience in a tonsillectomy. Now he said he thought the little girl had been operated on and lost something; he wondered what operations might come next, feared to open his mouth normally, and kept his hands over his mouth and stammered. Simple explanation of anatomy and physiology relieved the symptom quickly. Another boy began stammering when threatened with cutting off of the thumb because of persistent thumb sucking.

One must not forget that speech is probably the most highly integrated and sensitive of human functions. Therefore it normally and abnormally is affected by many stimuli. General emotional effects are universally seen. Stammering is a more specific syndrome, and one would expect a more specific etiology. To some extent this expectation is justified, but oversimplification of the problem is certainly to be decried. The causes are almost always multiple and complex. Neurologist, psychiatrist, teacher, and sociologist must coördinate their knowledge to attack such problems as stammering. The old-fashioned therapist riding one hobby is no longer tolerable.

REFERENCES

1. ORTON, S. T.: Reading, writing and speech problems in children. W. W. Norton: New York, 1937. 215 p.
2. SULLIVAN, H. S.: Conceptions of modern psychiatry. *Psychiatry.* 3:1. 1940.
3. FROESCHELS, E., JELLINEK, A.: Practice of voice and speech therapy. New Contributions and Voice and Speech Pathology. Expression Co.: Boston, 1941. 255 p.
4. CORIAT, I. H.: Stammering: a psychoanalytic interpretation. Nerv. & Ment. Dis. Monograph. New York, 1928. 68 p.
5. ROBBINS, S. D.: Stammering and its treatment. Boston Stammerers Institute. Boston, 1936. 121 p.
6. NIELSEN, J. M.: Agnosia, apraxia, aphasia. Los Angeles Neurol. Soc. Los Angeles, 1936. 210 p.
   A Textbook of Clinical Neurology. Paul B. Hoeber, Inc.: New York, 1941.
7. HEAD, H.: Speech and cerebral localization. *Brain.* 46:355–528. 1923.
8. WILE, I. S.: Handedness: right and left. Lothrop, Lee and Shepard Co.: Boston, 1934. 439 p.
9. LINDSLEY, D. B.: Bilateral differences in brain potentials from two cerebral hemispheres in relation to laterality and stuttering. *J. Exper. Psychol.* 26:211–225. 1940.
10. RANK, B.: Personal communication.

CHAPTER IV

THE FUNCTION OF THE FRONTAL AREAS OF THE HUMAN BRAIN [1]

> The highest centres, which are the climax of nervous evolution, and which make up the "organ of mind" (or physical basis of consciousness) are the least organised, the most complex, and the most voluntary.
> *Selected Writings of John Hughlings Jackson,*
> Croonian Lectures, March 1884.

IN SEPTEMBER 1848 Phineas Gage had charge of a road construction gang in Vermont. He had worked his way up to this position of foreman because his employers considered him energetic, persistent in executing plans, and shrewd. His associates thought him well balanced and "smart." All this suddenly ended on September 13. Gage was tamping a charge of powder into a hole drilled in rock; the charge exploded, and the tamping iron was driven upwards through his head, entering below the left malar bone and passing out through the cranium between the frontal bones. (See Fig. 13.) After months of severe illness with various draining wounds and abscesses, he recovered his strength, but he could not go back to his former work because of his change in personality. He became "irreverent, profane and impatient of restraint"; he was obstinate, yet capricious and vacillating. Taking to a roving life, he did small jobs here and there, finally showing himself as a freak by exhibiting the iron bar and his wounds. After twelve years he began to have convulsions which became more frequent and severe until he died after a fit in 1861. No satisfactory autopsy

---

[1] For a more extensive discussion and a full list of references, see my "Review of Neuropsychiatry" in the *Archives of Internal Medicine*, December 1941, and Freeman and Watts's book, *Psychosurgery* (C. C. Thomas, 1941).

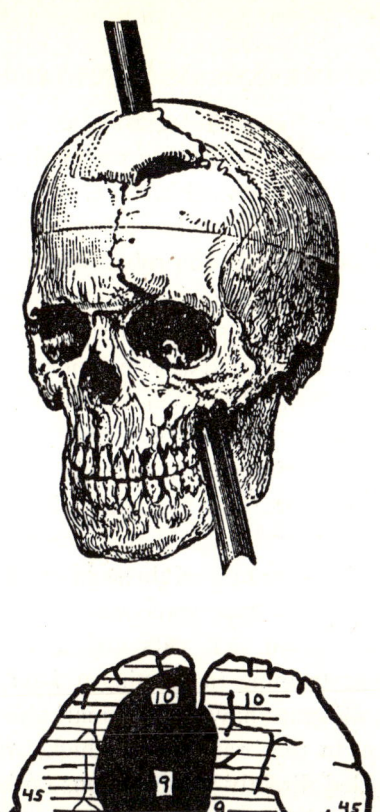

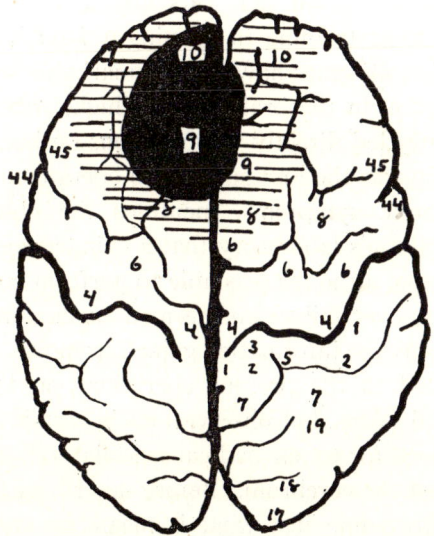

Fig. 13

The "crowbar skull," now in the Warren Museum at Harvard, as illustrated in Harlow's (1) paper in 1868. The instrument that went through the victim's head was really a smooth tamping iron 3 ft. 7 in. long and 1¼ in. in diameter. Beneath is a reconstruction, from observations on the skull, of the cerebral injury; those areas probably completely destroyed are black, the badly damaged are shaded.

was performed from the neurological point of view, but Dr. Harlow (1) succeeded in procuring the skull and bar for the Warren Museum of the Harvard Medical School. Inspection of these makes it evident that severe damage was done to both frontal lobes, areas 8, 9, and 10 probably being either actually removed (black area, Fig. 13) or put out of function bilaterally by contusion and infection (shaded area, Fig. 13).

This is the first well reported case in which a bilateral, frontal lesion of the human brain has been observed to cause changes in personality. Much animal experimentation has been done on dogs and monkeys. Some of this clearly forecast the results now found in the human. For example, Bianchi in 1893 after frontal ablations on monkeys said that the animals no longer showed any restraint or resourcefulness in small difficulties and that "utilization of past experience was absolutely wanting." Shephard in 1907 found that cats and monkeys lost recent memory, i.e., their training in opening a food box. Recently Fulton and his colleagues have done remarkable work on functional localization in the brains of the higher apes (2). This work apparently led directly to operations on human patients, for Moniz, who was the first surgeon to operate on the brain to remove psychotic symptoms, mentions the observations of Jacobson in Fulton's laboratory that a chimpanzee deprived of her frontal areas, although less able to perform complex tasks, lost her anxiety over failure and seemed much more placid.

It was not only the information gained from this experimental work which led to the present operations on the brain for agitated mental states, but observations in certain human cases where operations for tumor had caused bilateral damage to the frontal areas of the cerebrum. Before describing these cases it is important to define just what is meant by the anatomical term, "frontal area." The division of the brain into "lobes" is inexact and outmoded; frontal, parietal, occipital and temporal lobes are arbitrary morphological divisions with little biological significance. It is now known that many areas of the cortex are

FRONTAL AREAS OF THE HUMAN BRAIN

recognizable by physiological and histological criteria. When the cortex is mapped out in this way, the old division into "lobes" seems to be relatively meaningless.

The "frontal lobe" is usually defined as all of that cortex and white matter lying in front of the central fissure of Rolando (Fig. 14). This then includes the motor areas 4, 6, and 8, with

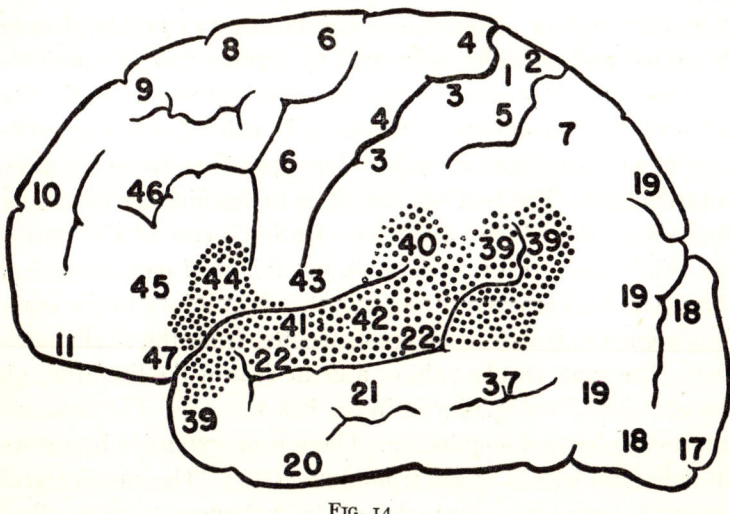

FIG. 14

Principal cortical areas, numbered according to the fields described by Brodmann on the basis of cellular architecture. The stippled areas are those concerned with speech. Areas 4, 6, 1, 2, 3, 5, 41, and 17 are "projection" areas, i.e., receiving stations or motor areas directly connected to lower centres by long projecting fibres. The frontal areas are 9, 10, 11, 45, 46, 47, and 32 on the mesial surface. Area 8 is more closely associated with the motor mechanisms of 6 and 4 than with the frontal.

the motor-speech area, 44, the frontal associative fields, 9, 10, and 11, and the triangular area, 45, with 46 above and below it 47, and on the mesial surface, area 32. These last seven constitute the "frontal areas," and the terms "frontal lobectomy" and "frontal lobotomy" are used as meaning the more or less complete removal or undercutting of areas 9, 10, 11, 45, 46, 47, and 32. The suffix "*pre*frontal lobe" seems to me illogical, in fact, linguistically ridiculous, since an area cannot be in front of the front, and because no anatomical fissure separates these seven areas off into anything like a lobe.

Because no cases are known where a normal man has been examined and then deprived of his frontal areas and reëxamined, the function of the frontal areas is not known accurately. Experiments on normal men are not allowed by our civilization. One must rely on observations concerning (1) brains already deformed and partially destroyed by tumors and (2) patients with mental symptoms who undergo cerebral operation for the relief of their symptoms. Obviously in neither case can satisfactory examinations be made before operation, so no scientific controls exist. The best one can do is to examine the cases and amass such data as are available. Harlow's case of the "crowbar skull" has already been cited, but this is of more historical than neurological interest, because the exact injury to the brain is not known, it had to be reconstructed from the skull specimen. The same can be said of a great deal of the literature on the effects of frontal injuries in the last war (3). The data are interesting but not convincing. There is an extensive literature on unilateral lesions of the frontal areas (4). The more careful observers have been able to detect slight changes in personality, loss of initiative, loss of the power of abstraction, and incapacity to resolve situations. Some authors even believe that they can localize symptoms to certain subdivisions within the frontal areas. For example, emotional disturbances are likely to follow lesions of the orbital surface of the frontal lobe (area 11) whereas intellectual deterioration results from injury to the lateral convex surface (area 10). Nevertheless, after reading of these numerous and extensive unilateral injuries one is most impressed by the lack of symptoms.

A recent monograph by Rylander (5) is superior to most of the previous work because careful psychological tests were carried out in cases with known operative lesions. He gives thirty-two thorough reports of patients in whom part of one frontal lobe was removed for tumor or (in three cases) for abscess; usually about two-thirds of the lobe was removed, i.e., areas 8, 9, 10, 11, and 45, but in some the excision was smaller. His follow-up examinations showed that in twenty-five cases there was "diminished inhibition of affective response," and in twenty distinct euphoria; fourteen patients showed restlessness and twelve a loss of initiative. Intellectual faculties were disturbed in twenty-one. These intellectual changes he specifies as: loss of attention in ten, slow thinking and "can't keep up" in fourteen, loss of memory for details in twenty-one, weak association in twenty, and poor memorization tests in eleven.

Six patients showed a marked increase in appetite and weight; in all of these there was also marked personality change. Rylander's conclusion is as follows:

> Mental changes occur after excision of parts of the frontal lobes. These changes are exhibited in alteration of personality. Generally they are not of such degree as to destroy the subject's ability to lead a normal social existence, but they can be fatal to persons doing qualified intellectual work. Consequently, it must be stated that the mental sequels, however important they may appear to the psychiatrist, do not represent any contra-indication to partial excision of the frontal lobes in urgent cases, when they are far outweighed by the advantages of a radical operation.

Reading this important monograph without studying the case histories would give one the impression that unilateral lesions of the frontal areas in either the right or left hemisphere frequently cause changes in personality and intellectual ability. A careful study of the case reports, however, reveals that in sixteen of the thirty-two patients there was probably damage to both frontal lobes, although only one was excised. Fourteen of these sixteen are cases where marked personality change was noted. Only six of the other sixteen cases showed personality changes; in this group the tumors were apparently unilateral and no evidence of compression of the opposite hemisphere was presented. Two of the six, however, had become epileptic since operation, and Penfield and Erickson have shown that diseased tissue remaining after injury may cause mental as well as epileptic symptoms.

Further evidence that brain tumors have a widespread effect upon the brain and cannot be looked upon as purely local lesions of one "lobe" is given by M. Harrower-Erickson (6). She applied the Rorschach test to twenty-five tumor cases on Penfield's service and found that there was a distinct abnormality of the personality, as judged by this test, in all cases with intracranial growths large enough to cause pressure and displacement. This was found in both operated and unoperated patients, and persisted for months and even years after operation. The change showed itself as a general restriction of responsiveness to psychological stimuli. The defect was slightly more marked in tumors affecting the frontal areas, but appeared almost as conspicuously in tumors of the parietal, temporal and occipital regions. These findings explain the old clinical observation that persons with brain tumor have a dull look, difficult to describe but recognizable to the experienced neurologist.

Four cases have been reported in whom frontal areas have been excised in order to remove a large tumor. The first and most carefully reported is Dandy's case; he operated on this man in 1930, and after prolonged and careful study Brickner (7) published the psychological observations in 1936. The areas removed were probably 8, 9, 10, 11, 45, 46, 47 on the left (see Fig. 15); from the right hemisphere a slightly larger excision was made, including probably a little more of area 8 and area 44. The results on the patient's mentality are given at length in Brickner's book; very briefly, the patient showed: (1) a limitation of the capacity to associate and synthesize, e.g., the patient showed distractability with impairment of selection, retention and learning; (2) impairment of restraint of emotion with boasting, anger and hostility; (3) additional symptoms such as impairment of abstraction, judgment, initia-

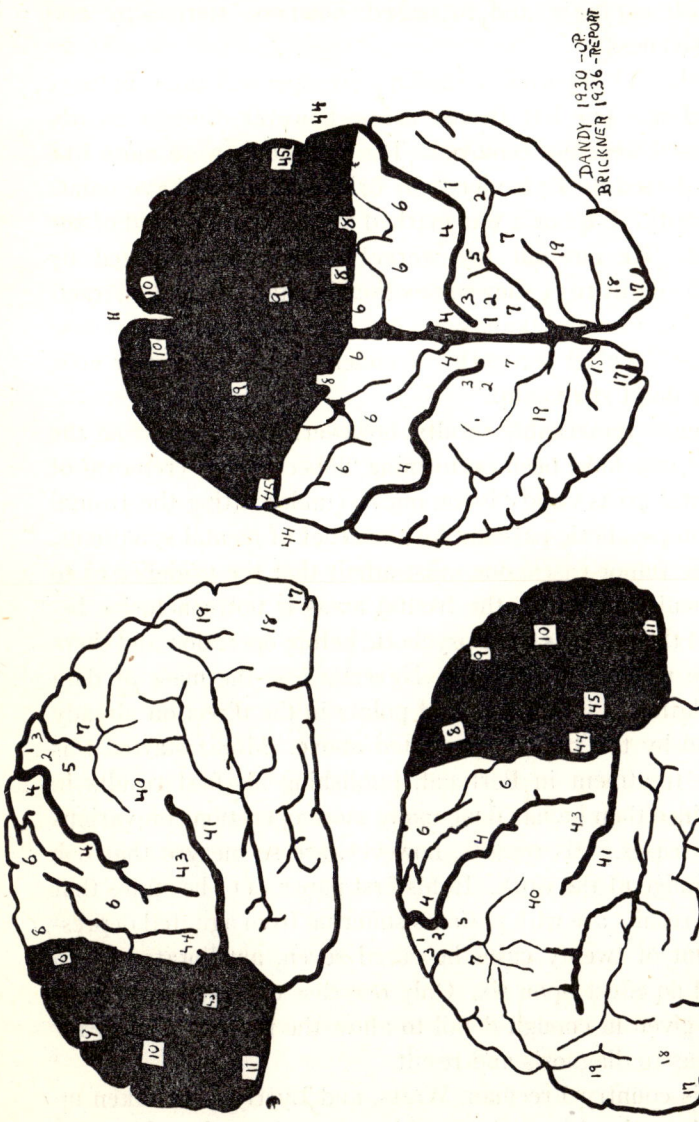

Fig. 15

Diagram showing approximately the amount of each frontal lobe removed by Dandy at operation in 1930, reconstructed from the description by Brickner in 1936.

tive, with euphoria and increased slowness, stereotypy and compulsiveness.

Ackerly (8) reported a similar case operated upon in 1933 by Spurling. The left frontal areas, however, though greatly compressed were not removed. The symptoms were more like those reported by Rylander than Brickner, but all have points of similarity. Euphoria was marked and the patient said of the surgeon: "He cut out my worry!" The case reported by Karnosh (9) in 1935 showed emotional instability and distractibility. David and Askanasy's (10) case is interesting because she remarked after recovery: "I understand things better now, but they don't stir me up."

The most remarkable results, however, have come from the surgeons who have been performing "lobectomies" (removal of the frontal areas) and "lobotomies" (undercutting the frontal areas) on psychotic patients for the relief of mental symptoms. As in the tumor cases, one must admit that the evidence as to the normal function of the frontal areas is not conclusive because all the patients were psychotic before operation and there could be no normal controls. Nevertheless, the mass of data accumulating is impressive and points in the direction already indicated by the tumor cases cited above. Moniz started this form of treatment in Portugal, publishing his first results in 1936; since then he has done many more operations on various types of cases. His reports, however, are so meagre that one cannot judge of the work. In his first paper (11) he states that the best results are with patients suffering from agitated depression. Out of twenty cases he cured seven, ameliorated seven and had no effect upon six. Only one case of the twenty, however, is given in enough detail to allow the reader to judge for himself as to diagnosis and result.

In this country Freeman, Watts, and Lyerly have taken up the work, and a few such operations have been done by other surgeons, notably Mixter (12), who in 1936 performed a bilateral "frontal lobectomy" on a boy for epilepsy and noticed afterwards that he lost his irritability and hostile attitude and became much easier to handle at home. From the published papers it would seem that Freeman, Watts, and Lyerly have done more than 125 "prefrontal lobotomies."[2] The results of their work are summarized in a recent monograph by Freeman and Watts entitled *Psychosurgery* (13). The book is a scholarly review of what is known about the frontal lobes in man. The authors' own cases, eighty in number, are used to illustrate the points under discussion; they are not reported in full. Summaries and tables present the main data from several points of view. Most interesting are the symptoms produced by this operation which separates the frontal areas of the cortex from their thalamic connections. In a series of 74 cases the following symptoms were most commonly produced:

Symptom	Total	Persistent	Temporary
Lack of initiative	73	30	43
Euphoria	60	22	38
Procrastination	56	29	27
Laziness	52	22	30
Facetiousness	49	18	31
Tactlessness	47	43	4
Increased appetite	70	50	20

A marked gain of weight occurred in about 40 per cent. There were many other symptoms that occurred frequently but were only temporary. These are difficult to evaluate because of the varying symptoms of the patient before operation, but the common picture for a few days after operation was that of a patient with rather expressionless face and monotonous "plateau" speech, dull and somewhat disoriented. This is explained as cerebral shock and wears off gradually. The usual permanent

[2] I cannot accept the term "prefrontal," as explained above, nor do I think that "lobotomy" describes this partial severing of the white tracts from the frontal areas. It would seem to me that "frontal leucotomy" would be a more descriptive name.

effects of the operation are described by the authors as follows:

Inertia and lack of ambition, reduction in consecutive thinking, loss of what is commonly called self-consciousness, indifference to the opinions of others, satisfaction with performance even though this may be of inferior quality and quantity — these may be considered among the primary results. Euphoria, evasion, bluffing, talkativeness, moria, aggressive behavior, teasing, indecent acts, inattention, poor judgment, — these might be classed among the secondary results.

Imagination is probably reduced quantitatively to some degree by prefrontal lobotomy, but even more important is the divorce between imagination and affect as it concerns the individual himself. What is accomplished by the operation is a separation of the ability of the individual to project himself into the future and the feeling tone that accompanies this. Moreover, it is especially the inner sensations, ideas, recollections, ambitions and disappointments, the regrets for the past and the fears for the future, that are particularly affected in this way.

Add to this the usual increased appetite and weight and the common persistent picture appears to be a patient often greatly relieved in regard to symptoms, but left fat, lazy, tactless, and a little silly. The secondary symptoms constitute more severe abnormalities of behavior, but they are more transient.

Looking at the picture from the other point of view, one can study what symptoms are relieved in these mentally sick patients by the undercutting operation. From the data given by Freeman and Watts, the symptoms most commonly present before operation were as follows, and were relieved as indicated in the percentages in parentheses:

"Nervous tension" (relieved in 72 per cent); "worry" (73 per cent); "depression" (75 per cent); "indecisiveness" (74 per cent); "insomnia" (70 per cent); "meticulosity" (95 per cent); "guilty feelings" (90 per cent); "agitation" (87 per cent). This is a notable list of unpleasant and incapacitating symptoms; they are, of course, largely the converse of the symptoms caused by "prefrontal lobotomy." To generalize from these observations is difficult; Freeman and Watts speculate as to "the relation of the self to the self," "imagination," "the capacity to project oneself into the future," and finally say of frontal lobe activities, "We believe they can be best summed up under the term 'foresight'." They postulate that the post-Rolandic cortex is concerned with memory, knowledge, and the past, while the pre-Rolandic is concerned with the projection of the whole individual into the future.

Their descriptions of the states seen after operation are admirably written, but the different character traits attributed to the frontal lobes leave one unconvinced that the authors have discovered any important psychological generalization. There is confusion because of wordiness and disregard of exact meanings. I find it impossible to work with such concepts as "egocentric," "extraverted," "imagination," and "self-consciousness" when attempting to describe neural functions; they are too complex. Nevertheless I find sentences and phrases here and there in the book that make me believe that the authors and I essentially agree as to what goes on in the normal frontal areas of man.

On page 313, speaking of the results of lobotomy, they say: "It is the capacity of foresight in relation to himself that is particularly lacking. It might well be that if the individual stopped to think, counted ten before he struck, the result would be different." They also mention on this page and again on page 298 that the symptoms caused by lobotomy are related to the *amount* of frontal cortex removed, not to any localization of the lesion. On page 315 they say: "The prefrontal regions long-circuit our actions, make for deliberation and delay, to the end that the decision shall be mature and the results measure up to expectation. They impose caution, restrain any action until we are as certain as is possible of the future implications of the action."

This formulation of the function as "long-circuiting" seems to me the essence of the problem. The idea is implicit in Sherrington's (14) theory of central nervous system integration; upon this basis one may explain higher mental functions. The terms may not be just those used to describe the lower reflex mechanisms, but they are similar. Indeed up to the present there is no hint of any fundamental difference between the "mental" and "non-mental" functions of the central nervous system, whether they be studied by chemical, physical, or microscopical methods. Even at spinal levels there is an anatomical and physiological mechanism which to me gives a clue as to the nature of such "mental" attributes as memory and learning. It is the mechanism that allows spread of impulses from one reflex level up and down to other segments, and by spread aids delay, and Fulton's (15) term, "long-circuiting" best epitomizes the idea. Short reflex arcs across the cord, medulla, or other lower centers give rapid automatic responses. These can be termed "short circuits." When a nerve impulse is shunted up the cord to higher levels — as most impulses normally are — then "long-circuiting" begins. It is the mechanism that allows for an enormous increase in association; it gives higher integration and leads to delayed action. This process of spread is essential for coördination. Its acme is found in the cerebral cortex where stimuli arriving at one receiving station (e.g., the visual "center") spread in innumerable directions to many other cortical areas, awakening associations, habitual responses, memories. Sherrington (16) refers to the cerebral cortex as "one of several bridges from input to output, though it is of them all the longest way round and the most complex." The longest way round would seem to be just what is needed to cause a delay in response, probably a most necessary and useful mental process, for while delay persists the spreading impulses are making more and more contacts, they are arousing more and more associations (17). This allows the past experience of the individual to affect his behavior, and if there is any distinction between man and "lower" mammals, it would seem to be this: adult man usually looks ahead and acts in the light of past experience, it is typical of his behavior that he "puts two and two together"; even in the highest apes this process is but rudimentary.

Freeman's theory that "imagination" and "foresight" are especially highly integrated functions of the frontal areas falls down at this point. A simple conditioned reflex is a kind of foresight; an animal learns that a red light will be followed by food, and secretes saliva in preparation for the expected food. This is the most rudimentary form of acting in the light of past experience; by the same token it is the simplest sort of foresight. Enough brain tissue is necessary to make reflex circuits of the sort we call "long-circuiting," but the frontal cortical areas are not necessary for such reactions. In fact no cortex at all is needed in lower vertebrates.

The fact pointed out by Freeman and Watts (page 298) that "there would seem in this material to be a certain quantitative relationship between the severity of the symptoms produced by operation and the amount of frontal lobes separated from the rest of the brain" is important. To my mind it suggests that the operation makes its effect by greatly reducing the number of possible circuits for association. The more destroyed the less "long-circuiting" remains. No specific trait or character of man is taken away. The essential point is that the extraordinarily extensive mechanism for association has been reduced. This is the mechanism described in Chapter II that makes man superior to all other animals and calls for the development of an extensive cortex, much of it non-specialized. The other observation of Freeman and Watts (page 298) that "the symptoms of frontal lobe deficit undergo gradual regression" is also in favor of my theory that the important thing for intellectual function is an immense number of paths for association, unspecialized but joining specialized cortical areas. Thus a patient who becomes regardless of the opinions of others and hypomanic after lobotomy may later reorganize his personality on the basis of what he has left in the way of association paths. This would explain improved behavior several months after operation. If the frontal lobes were the "centers" for 'foresight" or 'imagination," such improvement could never occur. The fact that it usually occurs after "prefrontal lobotomy" indicates that other cortical areas with unoccupied association paths can form the sort of reflex pathways that give the person "foresight." It would seem to me that a great richness of conditioned reflexes would do this. Memories related to specific situations are experience and make the basis of any action planned in the light of experience. To have planning, looking ahead and imagination, one needs no new mechanisms, only an extension of the association areas.

Why memories for long past events are never lost after injury to the frontal areas, I do not know. I believe that memory for recent events is impaired, but is soon compensated by other available areas taking on the job of registering the new associations. Perhaps remote memories become associated with so many cortical mechanisms that no one operation will obliterate them. I emphatically disagree with Freeman and Watts's conclusion that frontal areas have to do with the future (foresight, planning, imagination) and the cerebral cortex behind the central sulcus is a storehouse for knowledge. Their own cases prove to me that "foresight" is retained after frontal lobe injury and that memory is to some degree impaired.

In frontal lesions no especial quality of behavior is lost; it is more as if there were a quantitative deficit. The frontal areas (as well as some parietal and temporal areas of cortex) have the function of association. Stimuli reaching one or more of the receiving stations in the cortex (visual, auditory, tactile, etc.) spread rapidly through ever widening association paths to many areas of the cortex. This causes "long-circuiting" of the nerve impulses, there is delay in response, time and opportunity are given to the cerebral organ to respond to an outside stimulus in the light of past experience. This is the essence of intellectual function. It cannot be localized narrowly because its full effectiveness depends on its widespread topography and multiplicity of pathways. Lorente de Nó (18) has given a hint as to this complexity and its capacity of continued, "reverberating" function. Destruction of these "association areas," it seems to me, would give just such symptoms as the surgeons and their coworkers have described and in a quantitative way. What is needed is more observations of these patients by trained psychiatrists and psychologists before and after operation, who will present the data fully on each case.

From the standpoint of therapy, radical excision of parts of the brain to relieve mental symptoms calls for careful consideration. Is the surgeon justified in depriving a patient of the most important part of his intellect in order to relieve him of emotional troubles? In the results as interpreted by the "psychosurgeons" themselves it is seen that they usually leave the patient lazy and undiscriminating. In other words they often take away the highest integration ("conscience," or "superego," perhaps) in order to make the patient happier. In my opinion this is a justifiable procedure only when the patient is old and the prognosis hopeless. Specifically, I can only recommend the operation in cases of prolonged agitated depression over sixty years of age, or in rare instances in younger patients who show mental deterioration and neurological and electroencephalographic evidence of cerebral degeneration. To perform such an operation upon recoverable psychotic and neurotic states in people under sixty seems to me to be unjustified. I believe that practically all patients under sixty would refuse operation if *compos mentis* for a few moments so that they could be asked, "Would you rather suffer your present symptoms, perhaps for a period of years, or run a 50–50 risk of permanently losing your judgment?"

REFERENCES

1. HARLOW, J. M.: *Publ. Mass. Med. Soc.* 2:329. 1868.
2. FULTON, J. F.: Physiology of the nervous system. Oxford University Press: London, 1938.
3. GOLDSTEIN, K.: Significance of frontal lobes for mental performances. *J. Neurol. u. Psychopath.* 17:27. 1936.
   FEUCHTWANGER, E.: Die Funktionen des Stirnhirns. Julius Springer: Berlin, 1923.
   GRÜNTHAL, E.: Uber ein Bruderpaar mit Pickscher Krankheit. *Ztschr. f.d. ges. Neurol. u. Psychiat.* 129:350. 1930.
4. PENFIELD, W., EVANS, J.: Frontal lobe in man; clinical study of maximum removals. *Brain.* 58:115. 1935.
   FOERSTER, O.: Die psychischen Störungen der Hirnverletzten. *Ztschr. f.d. ges. Neurol. u. Psychiat.* 16:346. 1918.
5. RYLANDER, G.: Personality changes after operations on the frontal lobes. Oxford University Press: London, 1939.
6. HARROWER-ERICKSON, M.: Personality changes accompanying cerebral lesions. I: Rorschach studies of patients with cerebral tumors. *Arch. Neurol. & Psychiat.* 43:859. 1940.
7. BRICKNER, R. M.: Intellectual functions of the frontal lobes. Macmillan Co.: New York, 1936.
8. ACKERLY, S.: Instinctive, emotional and mental changes following prefrontal lobe extirpation. *Am. J. Psychiat.* 92:717. 1935.
9. KARNOSH, L. J.: Clinical aspects of frontal lobe disease. *J. Indiana Med. Assoc.* 28:568. 1935.
10. DAVID, M.: Tumeur sous-frontale bilatérale à symptomatologie affective; étude psychologique après ablation de la tumeur et des deux pôles frontaux. *Encephale.* 1:34. 1939.
11. EGAS MONIZ: Les possibilité de la chirurgie dans le traitement de certaines psychoses. *Lisboa med.* 13:141. 1936.
12. MIXTER, W. J., TILLOTSON, K. J., WIES, D.: Reports of a partial frontal lobectomy and frontal lobotomy performed on three patients: one chronic epileptic and two cases of chronic agitated depression. *Psychosom. Med.* 3:26–37. 1941.
13. FREEMAN, W., WATTS, J.: Psychosurgery. C. C. Thomas: Springfield, 1942.
14. SHERRINGTON, C. S.: Integrative action of the nervous system. London, 1911.
15. FULTON, J. F.: Muscular contraction and the reflex control of movement. Baltimore, 1926.

16. SHERRINGTON, C. S.: Selected writings of Sir Charles Sherrington. Hoeber: New York, 1940.
17. COBB, S.: A preface to nervous disease. William Wood: Baltimore, 1936.
18. LORENTE DE NÓ, R.: Limits of variation of synaptic delay of motoneurons. *J. Neurophysiol.* 1:187–245. 1938.

CHAPTER V

THE ANATOMICAL BASIS OF THE EMOTIONS

> Smells are surer than sounds or sights
> To make your heart-strings crack —
> They start those awful voices o' nights
> That whisper, "Old man, come back."
> That must be why the big things pass
> And the little things remain,
> Like the smell of the wattle by Lichtenberg,
> Riding in, in the rain.
> RUDYARD KIPLING, *The Five Nations*, 1903.

ANATOMICAL INTRODUCTION

BEFORE discussing the anatomical and physiological mechanisms that aid in the expression of emotions, it is necessary to review the anatomy of the autonomic nervous system and its relation to the glands of internal secretion. One cannot talk about emotions even in a simple way without frequently referring to these neurological and endocrinal data. Below is given a very short epitome of the main facts. For a somewhat longer description, see *Foundations of Neuropsychiatry* (1); details can be found in the monograph by White and Smithwick (2).

The autonomic nervous system is motor in its function and has two main divisions: the craniosacral ("parasympathetic") and the thoracolumbar ("sympathetic"). These are largely antagonistic: for example, the cranial autonomic supplies the iris with constrictor fibers, while impulses from the sympathetic fibers in the neck dilate the pupil. Figure 16 shows the anatomy in a diagrammatic way and indicates many other organs with balanced innervation. The cranial autonomic has varied functions: the vagus acts by slowing the heart, constriction of the bronchi, contraction of the stomach and intestine with relaxation of their sphincters, and by causing secretion in the stomach and pancreas; the glossopharyngeal and facial nerves carry

ANATOMICAL BASIS OF THE EMOTIONS

fibers controlling secretion in the salivary and lacrimal glands. The facial nerve also has vasodilator fibers which go to the cerebral vessels via the geniculate ganglion. Along with the oculomotor nerve run constrictor fibers to the iris.

Contrast with this list the functions of the thoracolumbar (sympathetic) division: dilatation of the pupil; protrusion of the eyeball; secretion of sweat; erection of hair; vasodilation and vasoconstriction; contraction of sphincters of anus and vagina; acceleration of the heart; dilatation of the bronchi; inhibition of intestinal peristalsis with closure of the pyloric and ileocecal sphincters; the contraction of the bladder is inhibited, while the sphincter is contracted; the liver glycogen is converted into glucose, and the spleen discharges red corpuscles. These are the best known, obviously they are emergency functions, called into play when strong emotion shows that the body is in need of its reserves.

The principal autonomic pathways may be enumerated as follows (see Fig. 16):

I. Autonomic Innervation of the Eye
  (a) Parasympathetic from cells in the midbrain. Function — accommodation and contraction of the pupil.
  (b) Sympathetic from cells in the spinal cord. Function — dilatation of the pupil and exophthalmos.

II. Autonomic Innervation of the Submaxillary Gland
  (a) Parasympathetic from cells in the hindbrain. Function — increases secretion and dilates vessels.
  (b) Sympathetic, from cells in the spinal cord. Function — to contract and dilate vessels of gland and increase salivation.

III. Autonomic Innervation of the Parotid Gland
  (a) Parasympathetic, from cells in the hindbrain. Function — to increase secretion of saliva.
  (b) Sympathetic, from cells in the spinal cord. Function — to increase salivation and contract vessels of gland.

IV. Autonomic Innervation of the Cerebral Arteries
  (a) Parasympathetic, from cells in hindbrain. Function — vasodilatation.
  (b) Sympathetic, from cells in the spinal cord. Function — vasoconstriction.

V. Autonomic Innervation of the Heart
  (a) Parasympathetic, from cells in the hindbrain. Function — cardiac inhibition and coronary constriction.

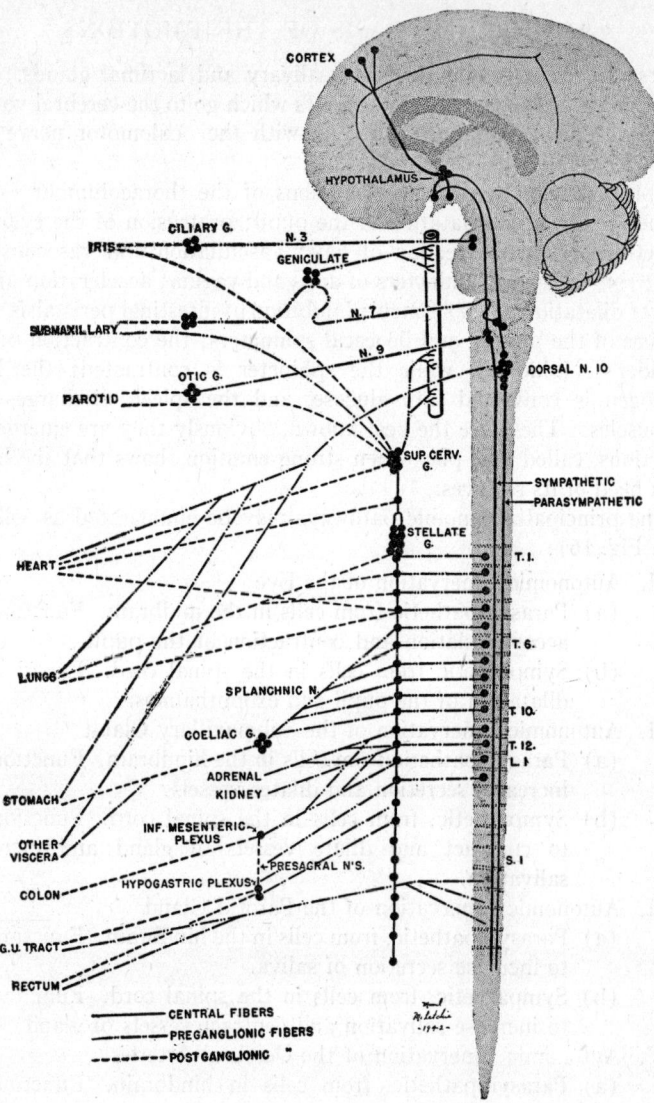

FIG. 16

Diagram of the main centers and pathways of the Autonomic Nervous System. The tubular structure parallel with the brainstem that receives fibres from the geniculate and superior cervical ganglia is the internal carotid artery.

G. = ganglion   N. = nerve

N. 3, N. 7, N. 9 = third, seventh, and ninth cranial nerves.

Dorsal N. 10 = dorsal nucleus of the tenth cranial nerve (vagus).

T. 1 = First thoracic nerve   S. 1 = First sacral nerve
L. 1 = First lumbar nerve   G. U. = genito-urinary

(Modified from Cobb *Foundations of Neuropsychiatry*, Williams & Wilkins, Baltimore, 1941.)

ANATOMICAL BASIS OF THE EMOTIONS

    (b) Sympathetic, from cells in the spinal cord. Function — cardiac acceleration and coronary dilatation.
VI. Autonomic Innervation of Lungs
    (a) Parasympathetic, from cells in the hindbrain. Function — constricts bronchi.
    (b) Sympathetic, from cells in the spinal cord. Function — dilates bronchi.
VII. Autonomic Innervation of the Musculature of the Stomach and Small Intestine (Exclusive of the Sphincters)
    (a) Parasympathetic from cells in the hindbrain. Function — to excite peristalsis.
    (b) Sympathetic from cells in the spinal cord. Function — to inhibit peristalsis.
VIII. Autonomic Innervation of Genito-urinary Tract
    (a) Parasympathetic from cells in the sacral spinal cord. Function — urination, defecation, vasodilation, and erection.
    (b) Sympathetic, from cells in the lower thoracic and upper lumbar cord. Function — to excite contraction of the internal sphincter, prostate, seminal vesicles; inhibits rectum and bladder.
IX. Autonomic Innervation of Arteries (exclusive of brain)
    (a) Parasympathetic neurons, probably from cells in the dorsal root ganglia of the spinal cord. Function — vasodilatation.
    (b) Sympathetic, from cells in lateral horns of cord T_1 to L_2. Function — vasoconstriction.
X. Sudomotor and Pilomotor Function of Skin are Served much as the Vessels in IX

The endocrine glands that obviously are related to emotional expression are, first of all, the adrenal and thyroid. Less directly one may name the pancreas, pituitary, parathyroid, and sex glands. I know of no relationship between the thymus and emotions, although the ancients spoke of "thymic temperaments," and the word "cyclothymic" is in common use to describe patients with periodic changes of mood. The ancients would have been nearer the truth had they picked out the adrenal gland as the great source of temperamental expression, for its internal secretion sets up that whole series of phenomena that are found with sympathetic stimulation — muscular tension, rapid heart, high blood pressure, wide pupils, erect hair, defecation, and urination. There is even shortening of clotting time in the blood. The animal is prepared for the emergencies of fight or flight.

Cannon (3) (4) has ably described this in his books, and has also proved the emergency nature of these reactions by showing that a cat can live with the entire sympathetic division of the autonomic system removed. It is important to remember that the adrenal is the only gland of internal secretion innervated directly by the spinal cord. Fibers from cells in the lateral horns of T_{10}, T_{11}, T_{12}, and L_1 go directly to the cells of the adrenal medulla. The only other endocrine gland that receives direct innervation of secretory mechanisms is the pituitary; this is innervated from the hypothalamus, causing an antidiuretic effect, and perhaps an increase in thyrotropic hormone. All the other endocrine glands are stimulated by hormones, other humoral substances or changes in blood supply, the latter being directly controlled by the autonomic system. Strong emotion affects the secretion of several of these glands, for example, the increase in sugar in the blood following fear and rage; hyperthyroidism gives a clinical replica of the fear reaction, even to the protuberant eyes and sometimes erected hair. Obviously the activity of sex glands is closely bound up with the tender emotions. Frustration of sexual drives is often associated with fear and rage.

Smell and Emotions

Poets are always years, if not centuries, ahead of scientists. They see and understand what goes on; the scientist labors along in the rear, trying to explain why it goes on. Of course the beginning of all science is objective description, and many poets were good, simple scientists of the old naturalist type. But it is a long step from the observation of an item of human behavior, with some intuitive insight into the implications, to the scientific explanation of the anatomy, physiology, and psychology behind the behavior. Scientific bits are laboriously discovered over the years until at last a partly fitted mosaic gives a clue to the nature of the whole picture. The poet sees the essentials in a flash and puts them into a form that makes others feel their truth and importance. If the observation is not a true one, the poet's admirers soon leave him, or only a few crackpots remain. It is when he "strikes to the heart of things" and says so in some universal symbolism that the poet lives.

But why is it the "heart-strings" that crack, and getting at the "heart of things" that affects us? Because the common experience of man has been that when he is suddenly faced with an emotional situation something happens in his left chest, something fundamental and connected with a vital organ. In fact he has felt his heart slow down, perhaps skip a beat, and then suddenly accelerate. Our language is full of terms that come right from visceral experience: "so scared he couldn't spit" (referring to salivary inhibition), "melancholic" (the black bile), "he has no guts" and "scared the shit out of him" (referring to intestinal results of fear), "it burned me up" (vasodilation), "white with rage" (vasoconstriction). There are a great many others, some of them more completely absorbed into the language, like the word "disgust," used largely in the abstract; originally it came directly from a bad taste in the mouth and its effect.[1]

Smell and taste are closely allied; in fact, most of what one calls taste is really flavor and aroma, with little relation to the four categories of taste — bitter, sweet, sour, and salty. Take, for example, this passage of prose that would make any child of the country nostalgic:

> To the boy Henry Adams, summer was drunken. Among senses, smell was the strongest — smell of hot pine-woods and sweet-fern in the scorching summer noon; of new-mown hay; of ploughed earth; of

[1] The psychosomatic relations are further discussed in Chapter IX.

box hedges; of peaches, lilacs, syringas; of stables, barns, cow-yards; of salt water and low tide on the marshes; nothing came amiss. Next to smell came taste, and the children knew the taste of everything they saw or touched, from pennyroyal and flagroot to the shell of a pignut and the letters of a spellingbook — the taste of A–B, AB, suddenly revived on the boy's tongue sixty years afterwards. Light, line, and color as sensual pleasures, came later and were as crude as the rest (5).

It is not mere coincidence that smells "hit us where we live" and that poets have appreciated the fact. In vertebrates below mammals practically the whole forebrain is devoted to smell. The brain stem, with its great motor and sensory nuclei and basal ganglia masses at the anterior end, is largely a reflex mechanism for seeing, hearing, touching, locomotion, and visceral control. The nuclei for the higher regulation of the heart, temperature, metabolism, respiration, and other visceral functions lie in the hypothalamic region, above the pituitary body and below the basal ganglia (Fig. 18). All sensory stimuli pass up to the thalamus, excepting the sense of smell. Motor coördinations are cared for in the other basal ganglia. In these lower vertebrates a very small and rudimentary area of the cerebral cortex is concerned with motor functions (6). The shell of forebrain that lies over and around the head of the brain stem is all primitive cortex (archipallium or old cloak). The neopallium is only developed in mammals.

The archipallium is almost entirely rhinencephalon (smell brain). The nerves from the olfactory bulb go directly to cortical receiving stations in the cingulum and hippocampus and to the amygdaloid nucleus. There is no relay through the thalamus as in other senses. Moreover, the olfactory centers mentioned above send fibres to form a large tract that ends in the hypothalamus (Fig. 19); apparently this has a controlling influence over these nuclei which in turn control so many visceral functions. The olfactory sense eventually has thalamic connections by way of a tract from the hypothalamus to the anterior thalamic nucleus (Fig. 21). Much more directly, however, it gets from its primary cortical receiving areas to the hypothalamus and visceral nuclei of the lower brain stem, including a close association with the taste centers. The evidence for a controlling influence of the rhinencephalon over the hypothalamus is presented in some experiments of Spiegel's (7) in which he cut the tract from rhinencephalon to hypothalamus as it approached the latter. The result was a cat that showed emotional outbursts much like the fits of sham rage brought out by Bard (8) when he removed the forebrain. (These operations are described in more detail below.)

Thus it is seen that the primitive cortex of the brain (archipallium) is largely an olfactory organ (rhinencephalon) that has not only elaborate receiving stations for the olfactory stimuli but also close connections with visceral functions through the hypothalamus. It is not merely a figure of speech when a man remarks that such and such an odor "aroused his passion" or "upset his stomach." The anatomical pathways are plain to see in lower animals. In man this old smell-brain lies deeply buried under the new cortex (neopallium), but it is not a rudimentary organ. Its central position is due to its early development and goes far towards explaining why "smells are surer than sounds or sights to make your heart-strings crack."

Emotional Expression

To discuss the anatomical localization of emotional reactions in a book on the "Borderlands of Psychiatry" may seem equally wide of the mark to those who consider psychiatry to be the "science of interpersonal relations" and to those who believe that psychology is not a "science" and physiology can explain all. To the former I will seem to be dealing with neurology; to the latter the cerebral centers under discussion will seem to be the very center of psychiatry, not a borderland. Both are correct in a limited sense.

It is obvious that much neurotic and psychotic behavior is

emotional. That is to say, there are visible facial expressions or motor acts, whether they be symbolic or realistic, which denote fear, rage, love, loneliness, sorrow, or their opposites. Besides this motor behavior of skeletal muscle which is innervated by the cerebrospinal nervous system, there is the behavior of smooth muscle and glands. Through these media the autonomic nervous system expresses emotion in heart rate and respiration rate (Fig. 17), intestinal and bladder movements, pupillary changes, sweating, flushing, pallor, and erection of hairs (Fig. 16). Functioning alone, none of these expresses much, except perhaps that most refined emotional discrimination expressed in the voice. Functioning together the cerebrospinal and autonomic nervous systems give unmistakable pictures of emotion. The grimaces of rage and fear are quite different from the facial expressions of love and sorrow. The effects on the viscera of these four major emotions are also different, although the symptoms overlap more than one would expect. If, however, one takes Cannon's point of view that the goal of these reactions is to keep the body from losing its equilibrium during stress, then some order can be made out of the phenomena. They are the physiological results of certain common environmental situations. The *emotions* are the *feelings* aroused by the stressful situations, typically described as rage, fear, sorrow, love, and loneliness, but often mixed.

Since one cannot observe the feelings nor make any record of them, it is necessary to be satisfied with describing the ways in which emotion is expressed. This is partly by the skeletal muscles by means of bodily movements, symbolic acts and signs, speech and voice variations in tone. But much more is expressed by the smooth muscles and glands in lacrymation, pallor, wide pupils, dry mouth, rapid heart, fainting, and heart stopping. In fear there is a special sweating of certain areas; the sugar content of the blood may rise; rapid respiration and deep sighs usually appear (Fig. 17); in the intestinal tract there is contraction; in the genito-urinary sphere, there is inhibition

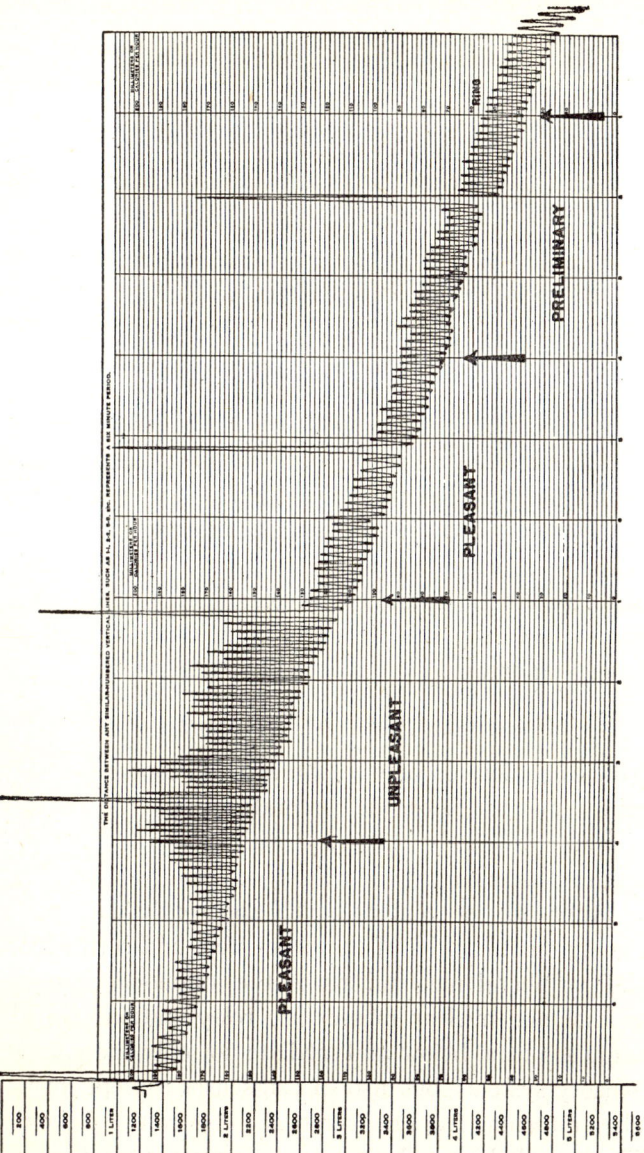

Fig. 17

Spirogram of a patient with neurotic anxiety who showed greatly increased respiration when she thought of unpleasant things. The long upward spikes are sighs. Upward lines indicate inspiration, downward, expiration. The record is from Finesinger's (18) investigation of respiration and its relation to emotion.

of sexual activity and emptying of bladder. In other words our viscera react strongly to emotions and use the "wisdom of the body" (4) to prepare for the emergencies of fear, hunger, and rage. But these are only some of the symptoms than can be seen and they apply largely to the emotions related to self-preservation and defense.

The group of tender emotions has to do with race-preservation. Love-making, mating, sexual acts, and the care of the young all come into this category. Here the physiological results are quite different. "Warmth," vasodilation, and salivation replace the cold sweat, pallor, and dry mouth of fear and rage. Many of the effects on heart, respiration, and gastro-intestinal tract are much the same, however, and, of course, the reactions of the genital mechanisms are quite special. In view of the discussion of smell above, it might be of interest to mention here the close association between odors and mating reactions. The turbinates in the nose and the areolar of the breasts have erectile tissue that responds to erotic stimulation as well as that in the genital organs.

Hypothalamus and Thalamus

In the diencephalon, or between-brain (the uppermost part of the brain stem) just below the cerebral hemispheres, are two masses of nuclei especially concerned with emotional phenomena. These are the thalami [2] and the hypothalamic nuclei (Fig. 18). The latter are the centers which apparently coördinate impulses going out to nuclei of the brain stem and cord which control the peripheral mechanisms of the autonomic system. The large thalamic nuclear masses are relay stations for all sensory impulses from below and mediate not only these great somatic sensory systems, but also special senses (except smell) and impulses returning from the cerebral cortex to the thalamic nuclei. The hypothalamus also sends an important tract to the

---

[2] *Optic thalamus* is the old term, but these nuclei have relatively little to do with vision except in one subdivision, the lateral geniculate bodies.

ANATOMICAL BASIS OF THE EMOTIONS

anterior nucleus of the thalamus; from here there is a relay to the cortex, so the hypothalamus has an indirect connection with the highest levels.

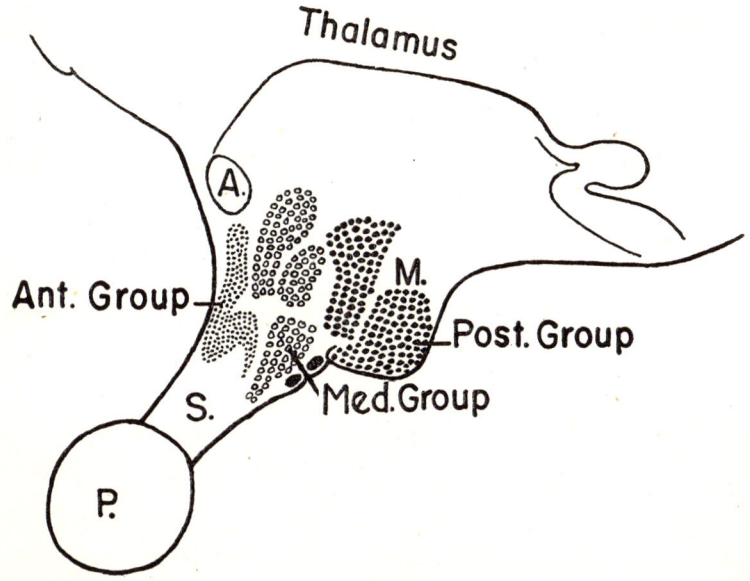

Fig. 18

Diagram of hypothalamic region (enlarged detail to elaborate Fig. 16) showing principal nuclear masses. The *anterior group* is made up of the anterior nuclei (which fuse anteriorly with the preoptic nuclei in front of the hypothalamus), the paraventricular nuclei and the suprachiasmatic nuclei (which are rudimentary in man). The *medial group* includes the lateral nuclei, and nearer the ventricular wall, the dorsomedial, ventromedial, posterior ventricular and tuber nuclei. The *posterior division* comprises the posterior nuclei and the four mammillary nuclei (medial, intermediary, lateral, and premammillary). A = Anterior commissure. M = Mammillary body. S = Stalk of pituitary. P = Pituitary body. For details of anatomy see Miller (19) and Rioch (20).

The hypothalamic control of mesencephalic, bulbar and spinal centers is by way of descending tracts to the tegmentum of the midbrain and upper hindbrain, to the lateral reticular formation in the lower hindbrain and to the anterolateral columns of the cord. There are also hypothalamo-hypophyseal and mammillo-tegmental tracts. Other connections are mammillo-thalamic (to anterior nucleus), thalamo-hypothalamic, pallido-hypothalamic, hippocampo-mammillary and vago-supraoptic. There is thus a close connection between the hypothalamus and other nearby nuclei, especially the thalamus and midbrain.

Evidence derived from animal experimentation can be divided into those observations which bear on (1) general reactions not localizable to any special nucleus of the hypothalamus, and (2) more localizable reactions which can be divided as follows:

ANTERIOR NUCLEI:
> *stimulation* causes contraction of bladder and stomach, gastric secretion, fall in blood pressure, increased respiration.
>
> *injury* causes erosion and hemorrhages into the gastric mucosa; loss of body regulation against heat; loss of water regulation (diabetes insipidus); hypoglycemia.

POSTERIOR NUCLEI:
> *stimulation* causes general sympathetic discharge with raised blood pressure, rapid heart, dilated pupils, hair erection, hyperglycemia, and decrease in gastric motility.
>
> *injury* causes somnolence, loss of sexual behavior patterns, like mating, loss of body regulation against cold, loss of hypoglycemic responses to cold.

LATERAL NUCLEI:
> *stimulation* inhibits gastric and bladder movements, increases respiration.
>
> *injury* causes obesity and somnolence.

Certain operations have been performed on laboratory animals that cause the symptoms of rage. Fig. 19 shows a diagram of a cat's brain with these operations indicated. In the first place Cannon and Britten (9) discovered that extensive injury to the frontal areas made the cat susceptible to spasms of rage-like behavior when disturbed (Fig. 19 lesion A). Bard (8) carried on this work and after much careful operating finally determined that the whole of the fore-brain could be removed along with thalamus and the anterior half of the hypothalamus

ANATOMICAL BASIS OF THE EMOTIONS

before the rage reaction was lost. When the posterior hypothalamus was injured, the sham rage never appeared again. In other words he located in these posterior hypothalamic nuclei the mechanism necessary to integrate the motor impulses into

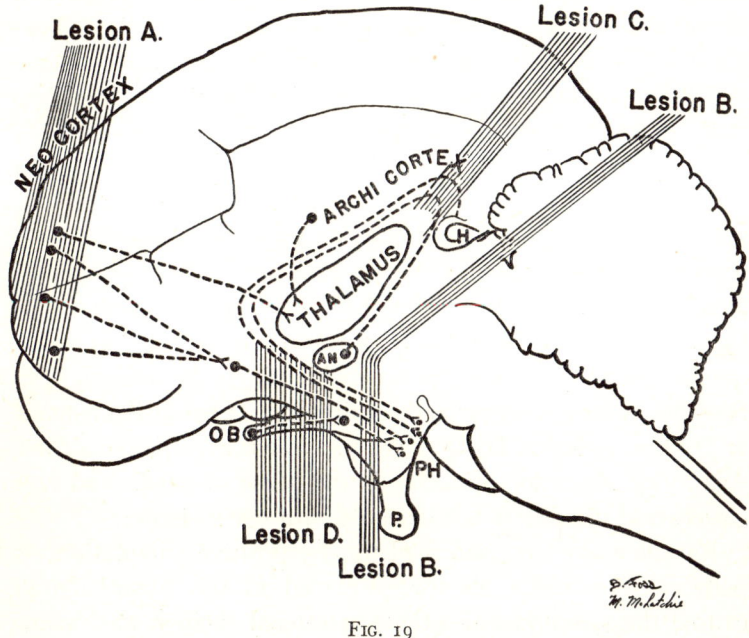

FIG. 19

Diagram of cat's brain showing various lesions that cause a show of rage. Lesion B transects the neuraxis in front of the midbrain and posterior hypothalamus (PH). Lesion C cuts the connections between Hippocampus (H) Amygdaloid nucleus (AN) and the hypothalamus. Lesion D cuts these two tracts and, in addition, tracts from the frontal areas and olfactory bulb (OB). P = pituitary.

the complex pattern we recognize as the expression of rage (Fig. 19 lesion B).

As already mentioned the sense of smell does not have a relay station in the thalamus like other kinds of afferent stimuli. Smell is transmitted from the olfactory bulb (OB) to the archicortex, laterally around to the cingular gyrus, hippocampus and amygdaloid nucleus and medially to the anterior perforated space whence a relay goes direct to the posterior hypothalamic nuclei (PH). There are also tracts from the hippocampus (H) and amygdaloid nucleus (AN) running without interruption to the hypothalamus but taking a long circuitous route around the ventricles and thalami back to their termination in the posterior hypothalamic nuclei, probably the mammillary bodies. Thus smell is closely connected not only with the vegetative centers which control autonomic motor behavior but also with centers that control movements of striated muscles. Bard's cats for example struggled, arched their backs, clawed, lashed their tails, snarled and moved their tongues besides showing all the sympathetic symptoms mentioned on page 76. Spiegel (7) has shown that when a small lesion is made at C (Fig. 19 lesion C) so that the tracts from the olfactory cortex and amygdala to the hypothalamus are interrupted, there results a state in which modified rage reactions can be elicited from the animal. The response is largely motor and respiratory. If the lesion is made at D (Fig. 19 lesion D) the rage response is even more marked. Again one sees how primitive is the sense of smell, and how closely and directly it is connected with one's viscera.

Ranson (10) has confirmed this by positive stimulation experiments in which electrodes placed in the hypothalamus caused the symptoms of intense emotional excitement — clawing, biting, salivation, erection of hair, and sweating. Gellhorn (11) has caused similar reactions by stimulating the mamillary bodies. No such reactions were elicited by stimulation of the thalamus, internal capsule or other neighboring structures. Examples of similar reactions in the human are seen in Foerster's case (12) (13) where the patient had manic reaction, flight of ideas and rapid talk when the surgeon manipulated a tumor that pressed on the floor of the third ventricle. Also Cushing (14) had a patient with glioma in the third ventricle region whose behavior was much like the sham rage in cats. Cushing calls this area "the very mainspring of primitive existence." Alvarez (15) even speaks of hypothalamic storms as related to

ANATOMICAL BASIS OF THE EMOTIONS 87

hysteria. Grinker (16) has stimulated the hypothalamus in man and caused sympathetic effects on blood pressure, pulse rate, respiration, and profound anxiety feelings with protracted sobbing.

This clinical evidence is interesting, but not convincing, because the experiments on the human are not sufficiently controlled. To clarify the problem, Masserman (17) has asked the question: "Is the hypothalamus a center of emotion?" And quite conclusively answered the question in the negative. His experiments are ingenious and crucial. In the first place he implanted a pair of bipolar electrodes in the hypothalamus of a cat and allowed this to heal in cleanly with wires coming out through the skin to be attached to a source of electrical stimulation. Then the cat was free and unanesthetized when stimulated; she reacted by crouching, growling, raising her back, and lashing her tail; there were biting movements of the jaws and the claws were unsheathed. On the autonomic side Masserman observed panting, salivation, wide pupils, and erect hair. The remarkable thing about all this vivid expression of rage was that it stopped instantly when the electrical stimulus stopped and the cat went right on with what she had been doing before the stimulation began, as if she had experienced no emotion at all. The activity induced was mechanical and stereotyped; it left no aftermath. In fact it differed so much from a true emotional state that Masserman calls it pseudo-affective. It seemed obviously to be a sham rage. Further proof was brought out by trying to "condition" the stimulus by the method of Pavlov. If electrical stimulation of the hypothalamus were accompanied by a subjective experience it should be possible to train the animal to produce the hypothalamic sham-rage by association with other stimulations. Stimuli such as intense light, voice, and air blast were used in conjunction with electrical stimulation of the hypothalamus. Such combinations of stimuli failed entirely in eight cats to bring out the expected conditioned responses. It thus seemed to Masserman that stimulation of the hypothalamus produced a syndrome of peripheral reaction unaccompanied by any subjective experience. In other words the motor expressions of an emotion were produced without any feeling.

Further proof of the correctness of this observation was reported in later experiments (17). Cats with similarly implanted electrodes were trained to light and sound stimuli so that they performed certain stereotyped acts (conditioned reflexes). They were then exposed to disturbing stimuli, causing the emotions of fear and rage. It was found that the recently learned conditioned responses were forgotten, extinguished by emotion. When the pseudo-affective stimulus was given (the direct electrical discharge into the hypothalamus) no such extinction of learned conditioned reflexes resulted. As soon as the current was turned off, the cat would react as well as ever to the light or sound. It seemed obvious that all the motor show of rage went on without emotional experience.

All of this is good reason for thinking that the hypothalamus is not a "center of emotion," of primitive feelings or feelings of any kind. It is a motor way-station where emotional expression is integrated into behavior patterns on its way out to the muscles and glands. Feeling, the essence of emotion, must take place elsewhere. Obviously this is a problem of awareness. But at what level does a mammal become aware of his sensory stimuli? There is good evidence that this takes place in a rudimentary way in the thalamus in man, and in a much more discriminative way in the cerebral cortex. The continuity of feeling with all its reverberating aftermath of strong emotion may be kept up by the thalamo-cortical circuits. But this is a question of "consciousness" to be discussed in the next chapter.

REFERENCES

1. Cobb, S.: Foundations of neuropsychiatry. Williams and Wilkins: Baltimore, 1941. 231 p.
2. White, J. C., Smithwick, R. H.: Autonomic nervous system. Macmillan Co.: New York, 1941. 469 p.

3. CANNON, W. B.: Bodily changes in pain, hunger, fear and rage. D. Appleton & Co.: New York, 1915. 404 p.
4. CANNON, W. B.: The wisdom of the body. W. W. Norton & Co.: New York, 1932. 312 p.
5. ADAMS, H.: The education of Henry Adams. 1905.
6. BAGLEY, C., LANGWORTHY, O. R.: The forebrain and midbrain of the alligator with experimental transections of the brain stem. Arch. Neurol. & Psychiat. 16:154–166. 1926.
   BREMER, F., DOW, R. S., MORUZZI, G.: Physiological analysis of the general cortex in reptiles and birds. J. Neurophysiol. 6:473. 1939.
7. SPIEGEL, E. A., MILLER, H. R., OPPENHEIMER, M. J.: Forebrain and rage reactions. J. Neurophysiol. 3:538–548. 1940.
8. BARD, P.: On emotional expression after decortication with some remarks on certain theoretical views. Psychol. Rev. 41:309–329; 424–449. 1934.
9. CANNON, W. B., BRITTEN, S. B.: Influence of motion and emotion on medulliadrenal secretion. Am. J. Physiol. 79:433–465. 1926–27.
10. RANSON, S. W.: Some functions of the hypothalamus. Harvey Lectures, 92–121. Williams and Wilkins: Baltimore, 1937.
11. GELLHORN, E., CORTELL, R., FELDMAN, J.: Autonomic basis of emotion. Science. 92:288–289. 1940.
12. FOERSTER, O., GAGEL, O.: Ein Fall von Ependymcyste des III Ventrikels. Ein Beitrag zur Frage der Beziehungen psychischer Störungen zum Hirnstamm. Z. ges. Neurol. Psychiat. 149:312–344. 1933.
13. FOERSTER, O.: Bumke u. Foersters Handb. Neurol. 5:2185. 1936.
14. CUSHING, H.: Papers relating to the pituitary body, hypothalamus and parasympathetic nervous system. C. C. Thomas: Springfield, 1932. 234 p.
15. ALVAREZ, W. C.: New light on mechanisms by which nervousness causes discomfort. J.A.M.A. 115:1010–1013. 1940.
16. GRINKER, R. R.: Hypothalamic functions in psychosomatic interrelations. Psychosom. Med. 1:19–47. 1939.
17. MASSERMAN, J. H.: The hypothalamus in psychiatry. Am. J. Psychiat. 98:633–637. 1942.
18. FINESINGER, J. E.: Effect of pleasant and unpleasant ideas on respiration in psychoneurotic patients. Arch. Neurol. & Psychiat. 42:425–490. 1939.
19. MILLER, H. R.: Central autonomic regulations in health and disease. Grune and Stratton: New York, 1942.
20. RIOCH, D. M., WISLOCKI, G. B., O'LEARY, J. L.: A précis of preoptic hypothalamic and hypophyseal terminology. Res. Pub. Assoc. Res. Nerv. Ment. Dis. 20:3. 1940.

CHAPTER VI

CONSCIOUSNESS

> Nothing is more striking in the history of science than the immense services that have been rendered at an early stage in the cultivation of every field by simple discrimination. . . . This first step which is often difficult and which may cost much effort of the imagination, lends meaning to observation, brings order to memory, thereby greatly strengthening it, and thus both directly and indirectly makes diagnosis easy.
> LAWRENCE J. HENDERSON, *Pareto's General Sociology*, 1935.

TO DEFINE "consciousness," to say what it is not, has for centuries been a main problem in universities and hospitals. All human beings, if normally developed, know perfectly well that they exist and constitute an organismal unit; more than that, they have a pretty good idea as to what they are like. When they use the word, "I," it connotes a certain sort of a person. Consciousness of one's ego is a matter of common knowledge, but like so many matters of common knowledge, it is a scientifically useless formulation until it can be better limited and defined. Probably most lower animals and possibly some plants have this feeling of being a unit, but they do not have highly developed brains that allow them to worry about the abstract aspects of the statement, "I am." Evidence on such subjects is almost impossible to obtain from organisms which cannot communicate, but some experiments, such as those on conditioned reflexes, strongly suggest that at least the vertebrates are constituted much as man is in this respect.

The discussion about consciousness has been confused mainly by two things; first, terms have not been defined and ambiguity has been the rule; second, the problem has been approached from different points of view. Miller (1) in his book on "Unconsciousness" has accepted sixteen meanings for the word "unconscious" which are in good use. This makes ambiguity such a menace to logic that he has been forced to the expedient of putting in parenthesis after the word "unconscious," every time he uses it throughout the book, the particular meaning of "unconsciousness" that he is then employing. He thus talks, for example, of "unconscious (unresponsive to stimulation)," "unconscious (unattending)," "unconscious (undiscriminating)," and "unconscious (unaware of discrimination)." This makes for clearness and really is the only practical way of writing on the subject.

The difference in points of view of the psychological schools that affect the meaning of the word is best illustrated by contrasting "unconscious," meaning "undiscriminating," with "unconscious," meaning "unaware of discrimination." The former is the sense in which the word is used by the behaviorists, who accept only objectively observable behavior. The latter is the sense accepted by introspectionists, who allow that subjective report is important. By the behaviorist awareness is admitted only if reaction is observed; by the introspectionists and the other more humanly oriented psychologists the experience of awareness is a basic fact of being.

From the point of view of the psychoanalyst, "conscious" and "unconscious" are quite opposite states and different from those signified when the word is taken in the senses used by academic psychologists. An "unconscious thought" is one repressed so that it cannot voluntarily be remembered and can only be brought up by hypnosis or the association technique. The confusion in meanings probably is partly to be blamed to bad translation of the word *Bewusstsein*, which is usually translated as "consciousness" but which in German has a connotation, a feeling of "knowing about," rather than meaning simply "aware of." There is an element of memory, so *unbewust* and *Unbewusstsein* — which is Freud's word for the state of mind arrived at when a painful event is repressed — might be translated, respectively, "forgotten" and "amnesia." The patient was usually extremely conscious of the event, but forgot it by a process of repression such that it might go on affecting his life and actions "unconsciously." If one wishes to use the term "conscious," *sub*conscious is a more accurate antithesis than *un*conscious for describing the mental mechanism, because the prefix "un" is too absolute to be accurate. There are various degrees of consciousness even within normal limits.

Thus one sees some of the main fronts along which the polemic rages. It is obvious that Henderson's "first step" (as described in the passage heading this chapter) has not been taken; the "simple discrimination" has not yet been discovered which would allow scientists to describe even tentatively the stuff of which consciousness is made. It is better, then, to take one point of view, to explore more in detail some common example. To go on in the philosophical discussion would merely increase the present multitude of words. Miller (1) has summarized both the academic and medical aspects of the subject most ably and gives a mass of references. The point of view of the present chapter is psychiatric and therefore medical.

SLEEP

The most common variant of consciousness with which we are all familiar is sleep. In that state most persons pass almost a third of their lives. They recognize the symptoms, welcome it at the proper time, know something of what it feels like to slide from "consciousness" to "unconsciousness," and have a wide experience in sleeping "well" or "poorly." Much is written about sleep by poets, essayists, and scientists — but despite the great prevalence of the phenomenon, almost nothing is known of its nature.

The physiological facts are few; good evidence points to the following as acceptable (2): There is no anemia of the brain and there probably is more blood in the brain during sleep.

The temperature of the body falls. The muscles relax, the amount of relaxation roughly paralleling the depth of sleep. Breathing becomes periodic and there is an increase of CO_2 in the blood and slight acidosis. The nerve cells of the central nervous system become less irritable and the electroencephalograms show characteristic changes. These observations seem meager and scattered when one considers how much investigation has been done from the very beginnings of physiology to elucidate the mystery of sleep. They do not coördinate to point to one theory of sleep. The phenomenon that shows the most accurate parallel with variations in sleep is the variation in the electrical potentials (electroencephalogram). Recent work by Davis and Loomis (3) has brought this out to a degree that makes one hopeful that here at last may be a method that will lead to a better explanation.

A subject with electrodes attached to the scalp is put in a situation conducive to sleep and the electrical potentials produced by the active cells of the cerebral cortex are recorded on a continuous moving paper for several hours, while the subject goes through various phases of sleep. For most of the observations the leads from the occipital lobes are best, because from here come off the regular "alpha waves" in a large proportion of normal persons. When drowsiness or the "floating state" sets in, the alpha rhythm becomes less regular and as light sleep comes on the alpha waves may group themselves into spindles with spaces between where waves are small or absent. As sleep deepens, some slower waves appear (6 per second), and in really deep sleep, long, slow waves replace the faster rhythm. (Fig. 20.) These may be as slow as one or two per second and of high voltage. In the deepest sleep, even these tend to disappear and the electroencephalogram is almost a base line with a few small waves. Sudden awakening immediately brings back the normal rapid rhythm associated with alertness. If deep sleep is disturbed, the long slow waves may be modified to resemble those seen in going into light sleep. Patients in coma from one cause or another will show the long waves of deep sleep, but they cannot be aroused.

An interesting experiment of Loomis' gave proof of a long-held theory — that subjects in sleep are still able to discrimi-

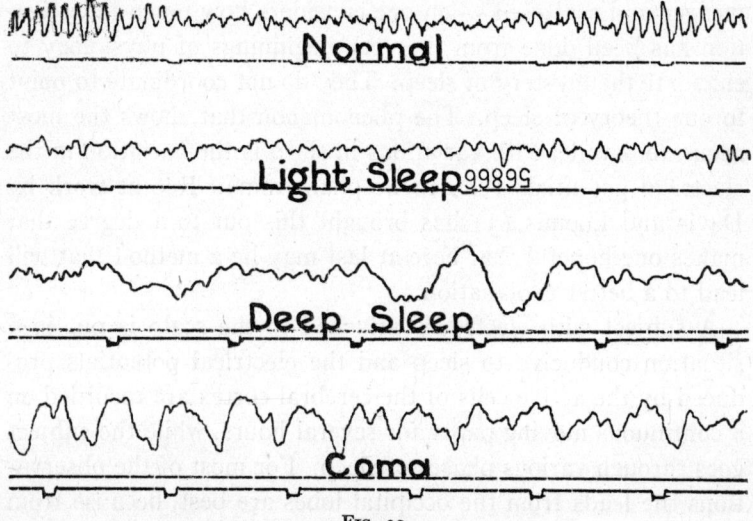

FIG. 20

Electroencephalograms taken from patients with varying degrees of awareness of environment. The waves of deep sleep and coma resemble somewhat the slow waves of epilepsy (see Fig. 23).

nate between stimuli. It has long been observed that a mother will wake at the slightest cry of her child when much louder noises do not seem to disturb her. Loomis showed that loud automobile noises outside the house had no effect upon the electroencephalogram of a sleeper, while a slight noise in or near his room, especially the slight snap made by pressing an electric switch, would start a change in the sleep waves towards the waking type.

All this goes to show that sleep can be described as having varying levels with characteristic electrical phenomena at each level. Moreover, when a person is asleep he is not unconscious (unresponsive to stimulation or undiscriminating); he is partly conscious all the time, because in all but the deepest level he is capable of discriminating between stimuli and because he is able to keep a sense of elapsed time and wake up according to order. Also, dreaming takes place and dreams that are remembered cannot be described as "unconscious" phenomena. They are retained and brought forth in the waking state. The content of dreams is certainly less censored by a repressive conscience, but, accurately speaking, this has nothing to do with unconsciousness. It has to do with being less inhibited, less aware of one's environment, less awake to the opinions of others, but more or less consciousness is necessary.

Physiologically speaking, there is some interesting data on where sleep control is located in the central nervous system. Bremer (4) operated on cats and was able to cut completely through the midbrain and keep the animal alive. The head of the animal then showed all the phenomena of sleep, such as closed eyes for rhythmic periods, and the electrical potentials from the cortex resembled those of sleep. It seems probable that the cat's brain went to sleep because no stimuli could reach it from the brain stem and spinal cord. All these stimuli were cut off from reaching the thalamus, which is the great sensory relay station in the base of the brain whence sensory impulses are redistributed to the cortex.

Probably the thalamus has a good deal to do with wakefulness and sleep, because not only do impulses of a sensory nature go to the cerebral cortex from the thalamus, but circuits come back from cortex to thalamus. The probability is that once the cortex is aroused by a shower of stimuli a reverberating circuit (to use Forbes's (5) original conception) is set in action and the short stimulus sets up a long-lasting state of vigilance or alertness. The physiological possibility of this mechanism has been proven by Lorente de Nó (6) and the psychological implications are well described by Campion and Smith (7). It would seem a reasonable speculation at present to say that the thalamus is important for consciousness, that a simple, undiscriminating awareness is possible at this level in mammals and that the cortex makes possible a more discriminating consciousness. The close connection of thalamus and cortex, by way of the reverberating circuits, supplies the mechanism for more lasting states of consciousness.

Figure 21 diagrammatically represents how all this might take place. Sensory pathways from the spinal cord (spinothal.) and the brain stem just above go to the great ventral nucleus of the thalamus. Nearby in the ventrolateral nucleus is received the large motor-coördinating pathway from the cerebellum. Visual (optic) and auditory tracts run to the lateral and medial geniculate bodies of the thalamus, respectively. From each of these nuclei impulses are relayed over new neurons to the cortex. The ventral nuclei send largely to cortical areas 1, 2, 3, and 5; the ventrolateral nucleus, with its tract coming in from the cerebellum relays, as one would expect, to the motor areas 4 and 6. The lateral geniculate sends fibres to area 17 and the medial geniculate to area 41 in the transverse temporal lobe. Thus primary sensory stimuli reach their highest reception levels. The lateral thalamic nucleus (L) sends tracts to areas 7 and 39, but the lateral nucleus is not connected directly with any cord or bulbar sensory tracts; its stimuli are relayed by association tracts from other nuclei in the thalamus, so the function of the thalamo-cortical neuron could be expected to be more complex. Apparently it is so, as lesions here indicate that the tracts have to do with the appreciation of the body scheme, a sort of global understanding of all the proprioceptive sensations, brought into a unit so that the limbs seem to belong to the body and to each other as a working whole. Lesions of these tracts cause anosognosia and autotopognosia (8).

From the medial nucleus (M) a large tract goes to the frontal areas 9 and 10. These are the tracts supposed to be so important in keeping up the tension states relieved by the opera-

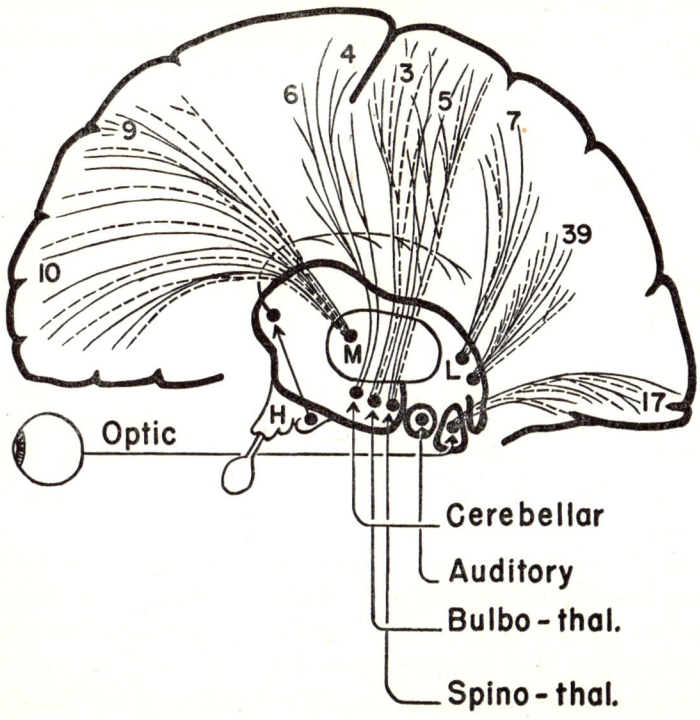

Fig. 21

Schematic representation of connections of the thalamus. *Optic* nerve fibres go to lateral geniculate body and from there other fibres pass to area 17; the solid lines represent these thalamo-cortical efferent fibres, the dotted lines represent cortico-thalamic fibres sending impulses in the opposite direction to make a "reverberating circuit." *Cerebellar* tract goes to ventrolateral nucleus of the thalamus, and relays go on to motor area 4 and 6. *Auditory* path ends in medial geniculate body and is relayed to area 41 in the temporal lobe which cannot be shown in this figure. *Bulbo-thal.* represents the paths to the ventral nucleus of the thalamus from the trigeminal nucleus and the dorsal nuclei of the bulb (gracile and cuneate). *Spino-thal.* represents the main sensory inflow from the cord to the ventral nucleus of the thalamus and thence relays to areas 3 and 5. Short fibres connect the different thalamic nuclei (not shown) so sensory and other impulses by a more indirect route reach areas 7 and 39 from cells in the lateral nucleus (L). From M, the medial nucleus, a large tract goes to and returns from the frontal areas 9 and 10. H, the hypothalamus, is connected with the anterior nucleus of the thalamus. Thence there is a tract to the olfactory cortex.

tion of "prefrontal lobotomy," described in Chapter IV. An area in the anterior nucleus receives fibres from the mammillary bodies of the hypothalamus and sends on a relay to the cortical areas nearest the old smell-brain (cf. Figs. 19 & 21). There are also tracts from the medial nucleus to the basal ganglia, and complex internuclear association fibres within the thalamus.

The possibility that there are reverberating circuits (5) from thalamus to cortex and back has been explored by several authors (7) (9) and makes an attractive hypothesis to explain a continued state of neural vigilance, awareness of self and environment or "consciousness." The possibility is made more of a probability by the finding of corticothalamic fibres paralleling the thalamo-cortical tracts just described. These are shown in Figure 21 as dotted lines from cortex to thalamus alongside of the solid lines going in the opposite direction.

Experiments on decorticate dogs and cats have shown that they can discriminate between stimuli in a simple way; the reactions are not "purely reflex" but involve past experience and conditioning. For instance, a barking dog will arouse rage reactions in a decorticate cat (1). The function of the thalamus in man in relation to consciousness, however, is probably much greater. A stimulus reaching the thalamus may be relayed to the cortex and set up an acute alertness that is continued for some time. The original stimulus may be visual, or tactile, or any sensation, but it gets its meaning through cortical associations and its ability to continue by the thalamic circuits. An important precursor is stimulation of the thalamus by the hypothalamus. Ranson and Magoun (10) have shown that here lies a "waking center" that probably bombards the midbrain nuclei and higher thalamic centers with stimuli. As soon as these stimuli are shut off, sleep is likely to supervene. Thus the vegetative centers below have a marked effect on the whole mechanism, and such factors as metabolism, fatigue, sleep rhythm, and circulation have a means of affecting consciousness profoundly (see Chapter V). This is not the only means of keeping an organism awake and alert; any of the afferent tracts from peripheral sense organs to the thalamus (Fig. 21) can equally well bombard the thalamus with exciting stimuli. Chief among these are the proprioceptive stimuli from tense and contracting muscles, for nothing puts one asleep so fast as complete relaxation (2), and muscular exercise is the best thing to keep one awake.

Thus it is seen that there is physiological evidence to show how sleep, wakefulness, awareness, and "consciousness" are integrated at various levels in the central nervous system. Likewise there is a mass of psychological data to show that consciousness (awareness and ability to discriminate) is not at all a matter of all-or-none (conscious or unconscious) but a matter of degree. If black signifies unconsciousness and white full consciousness the intermediary scale of grays indicates the states in which one mostly lives. Even when "normally" alert and interested, one is not conscious of many stimuli; in fact, attention keeps one from being reactive to the thousands of unimportant stimuli. An experiment by Morton Prince (11) proves this: He introduced one of his hypnotizable subjects to a stranger in his waiting room, then calling the subject into his office he asked him to write down everything he had noticed about the stranger. The list was a short one of the usual sort — hair, eyes, necktie, suit. Under hypnosis, however, Prince soon recovered from this subject a long and most remarkably accurate list of details: the number of buttons on waistcoat and sleeve, the exact stripe of the suit, the shoes and socks, facial peculiarities, etc. These had all registered during the brief interview, but had been outside of the focus of attention and so had been ignored. Riggs's (12) figure of the searchlight of attention shining upon the sea of consciousness, with sharp consciousness only in the bright light, makes a good teaching metaphor. Without this ability to attend to certain stimuli and disregard others a person would be useless; he would be in a continuous state of hypomania. In fact, starting with this as the acme of clinically known consciousness, one could arrange the various levels as follows:

Levels of Wakefulness

MANIC (distractible)
HYPOMANIC (coffee, benzedrine, etc.)
EXCITED but capable of attention ("go getters")
NORMAL responsive to environment (but selective)
ABSENT MINDED
DULL (phlegmatic)
STUPOROUS
COMATOSE
DEAD

The states above normal are to some degree pleasurable, at least exciting; the use of drugs such as caffeine and benzedrine bring about brief and mild hypomanic states. The dull states below normal are caused by so many disorders, psychological and neurological, that they are not even listed. The point is that between the manic state, where one is incapacitated by a too alert consciousness, and the oblivion of death, there is a continuous series of overlapping states. It is not a matter of *are* you conscious but of *how* conscious are you?

My personal belief is that consciousness (awareness of self and of environment) is not a theory, not "mind," not an abstraction that can be affected by discussions and new definitions. It is a function of nervous tissue in action, just as much as contraction is a function of muscle. It varies in degree according to physiological laws. It is observable by introspection (our best and ever-present proof of its reality) and by experiments on other persons and laboratory animals. At present there is no means for the simple description of consciousness. That first step has still to be taken by some imaginative physiologist or psychologist, and like all great steps, it will surprise the rest of us because it looks so simple. My guess just now is that consciousness will sooner or later be described in terms of electronic activity, as is suggested now by the electroencephalogram where alert consciousness seems to be associated with small fast potentials and deep unconsciousness with large slow potentials. Henry Head (13) must have had some inkling of this sort of varied activity when he described "neural vigilance" as changing and moving throughout the central nervous system. But no good metaphors should satisfy us. What is needed is a method that will quantitatively determine the amount of some physicochemical process that parallels what we already know as "consciousness."

REFERENCES

1. MILLER, J. G.: Unconsciousness. John Wiley & Sons: New York, 1941. 329 p.
2. KLEITMAN, N.: Sleep and wakefulness as alternating phases in the cycle of existence. University of Chicago Press, 1939. 638 p.
3. DAVIS, H., DAVIS, P. A., LOOMIS, A., HARVEY, E. N., HOBART, G.: Human brain potentials during the onset of sleep. *J. Neurophysiol.* 1:24–38. 1938.
   DAVIS, P. A.: Effects of sound stimulation on the waking human brain. *J. Neurophysiol.* 2:494–499. 1939.
   LOOMIS, A. L., HARVEY, E. N., HOBART, G. A.: Disturbance-patterns in sleep. *J. Neurophysiol.* 1:413–430. 1938.
4. BREMER, F.: Nouvelles recherches sur le mécanisme du sommeil. *Compt. Rend. Soc. de Biol.* 122:460–464. 1936.
5. FORBES, A., COBB, S., CATTELL, M.: Electrical studies in mammalian reflexes. III. The immediate changes in the flexion reflexes after spinal transection. *Am. J. Physiol.* 65:30–44. 1923.
6. LORENTE DE NÓ, R.: Limits of variation of the synaptic delay of motoneurons; synaptic stimulation of motoneurons as a local process; analysis of the activity of the chains of internuncial neurons. *Jour. Neurophysiol.* 1:187–245. 1938.
7. CAMPION, G. C., SMITH, G. E.: Neural basis of thought. Harcourt Brace: New York, 1934. 137 p.
8. NIELSEN, J. M.: Disturbances of the body scheme. *Bull. Los Angeles Neurol. Soc.* 3:127–136. 1938.
9. KUBIE, L. L. S.: Theoretical application to some neurological problems of the properties of excitation waves which move in closed circuits. *Brain.* 53:166–177. 1930.

10. Ranson, S. W., Magoun, H. W.: Hypothalamus. *Ergebn. d. Physiol.* 41:119. 1939.
11. Prince, M.: Personal communication.
12. Riggs, A. F.: Talks to patients, privately printed. 1915.
13. Head, H.: The conception of nervous and mental energy. *Brit. J. Psychol.* 14:126–147. 1923.

CHAPTER VII

CONCERNING FITS

> And one of the multitude answered and said, "Master, I have brought unto Thee my son, which hath a dumb spirit; and wheresoever he taketh him, he teareth him: and he foameth, and gnasheth with his teeth, and pineth away ... and ofttimes it hath cast him into the fire, and into the waters, to destroy him: but if thou canst do any thing, have compassion on us, and help us."
>
> Mark IX: 17–22.

THIS description written 1900 years ago depicts the situation in a family cursed with epilepsy. Demoniac possession was the theory as to etiology, and Jesus was asked to cast out the devil. Today the same sad group enters the physician's office. Father, mother, and child with the same plea, "if thou canst do anything." Long years of research have gone into the treatment of epilepsy and, thank God, the physician now can do much. But it takes a physician who does not narrowly specialize, who works in the borderlands between neurology, psychiatry, medicine, and surgery. And such a student of epilepsy will be richly repaid, for a wide clinical experience in studying fits brings with it experience with almost every type of neurological and psychiatric disorder.

Many fits are, of course, normal phenomena. Anybody can have a fit of weakness from laughing, but when muscular weakness repeatedly follows sudden amusement, it is called "cataplexy." Similarly fits of sleeping, twitching, muscle spasm, faintness, "absent-mindedness," bad conduct, and confusion are common enough. It is only when they become habitual, uncontrollable, or cataclysmic that they deserve the medical names given to fits: narcolepsy, convulsion, syncope, lapse, and fugue

— to choose some of the simple ones. How to distinguish the normal from the abnormal and pick out the neurological case, the psychiatric, the medical, and the surgical — that is the problem of the epileptologist. Today he must be able to apply the routine examination of all these four departments of medicine, and he must have the help of x-ray, electroencephalographic, and other laboratories. In a chapter such as this I cannot go into all the ramifications of this complex subject; two recent books cover it admirably: Lennox's *Science and Seizures* (5), and *Epilepsy and Cerebral Localization* by Penfield and Erickson (3). I will merely take up some aspects that seem important, to emphasize the borderland position of this scourge that affects over half a million people in the United States today (see Fig. 1B, page xii).

There is no better place to study "consciousness" than a clinic for epileptics. Here the interested person will see many and fascinating variations of consciousness, from the brief lapse lasting a few seconds, shown only by a blank stare, to the confusion states lasting for hours or the deep stupor following a generalized convulsion. In fact, some change in consciousness is part of every epileptic seizure (except the focal motor attacks affecting one side, and when these spread to become generalized, consciousness is affected). Moreover, the attacks of epilepsy are repeated and usually much alike in any one person, the same pattern sometimes reappearing for years. The investigator, therefore, can observe different types and degrees of impaired consciousness and lay plans for their study.

Many epileptics live a long life without ever having a convulsion. This will seem a surprising statement to those who do not realize that a convulsion is simply the motor manifestation of severe epilepsy. Some patients suffer only spells of dizziness or the short lapses of consciousness known as "petit mal"; these lapses may be accompanied by a turning or jerking of the eyes and head, but they are brief and certainly do not deserve the name convulsion. Nevertheless, there is no line that can be drawn between "petit mal" and "grand mal" because any epileptologist of experience has seen all sorts of gradations between the two: lapses with falling, lapses with wetting and falling and varying degrees of motor phenomena, until "grand" and "petit" becomes a distinction without a difference. The terms should be reserved for the extremes, admitting that the intergradations are common.

There may be sensory fits of all sorts; the commonest are visceral feelings of a vague nature, but vision, hearing, smell, touch, and pain may be implicated. Frequently these fits are only the precursor ("aura") of motor manifestations. Psychic fits are also varied; not only is the lapse of consciousness (described above) a psychic phenomenon common to almost all seizures, but there may be strange variations lasting a few seconds, minutes, or hours, such as dream states, feelings of "experiencing all this before" (*déjà vue*), confusions, rages, fugues, and ecstasies. Even the motor aspects of fits are very different. A common sort of fit is the major convulsion beginning with steady and extreme muscular spasm which is more and more interrupted so that the muscles begin to jerk and throw the limbs and body about (1). Relaxation into a state of limp coma follows. But by no means, as the textbooks aver, do all motor fits show "tonic" and "clonic" phase followed by "flaccidity." A very common type is made up of well coördinated movements repeated in an automatic, stereotyped way while the patient looks bewildered. These are often misnamed "hysterical" because the patient's acts seem to be purposeful in a crude way, but they are just as involuntary as the convulsion. Closer to the convulsion is the "coördinated epilepsy" of Rosett (2), in which cinema photographs of the fit show that the arms and legs are making running or other coördinated movements, not primitive jerks. Related to these are the postural fits, where the muscles contract in slow spasms and pull the body into certain postures but do not break down into clonic jerks. Last and most interesting is the focal motor attack, always beginning unilaterally in a given group of muscles and spreading by a motor "march" to other near, and then distant, muscle groups. This is the "Jacksonian" attack that usually signifies a lesion near the motor cortex.

Thus the abnormal neuronal discharge causes many and varied symptoms depending on where it arises and how it spreads in the brain. Penfield and Erickson (3) give excellent clinical and physiological data on cortical localization. But what is the "neuronal discharge"? To Hughlings Jackson it was a theory; to recent neurophysiologists (4) (5) it is an episodic and paroxysmal outburst of high-voltage electrical potentials in the brain which register on the electroencephalograph as rapid spikes, high slow waves, or combinations of these. The electroencephalograph has become the best objective measure of what is going on within the brain of an epileptic. Probably no epileptic seizure can take place without the accompaniment of "storms" of "brain waves." That the waves cause the seizures cannot be stated. Causality is a complex matter. Probably some physicochemical change in the nerve cells causes both the electroencephalographic waves and the clinical fit. This change is obviously *both* structural (in that chemical structures change within the cell) and functional (in that function is altered in a way that can be observed and recorded).

In the light of these main facts about fits, epilepsy may be defined as follows:

Epilepsy is a disorder of the brain that causes repeated episodes in which the usual functional abnormalities are: (1) changes in the electrical potentials as seen in the electroencephalogram; (2) changes in consciousness; (3) nervous discharge into smooth muscle, striated muscle, or glands, causing involuntary visceral or motor behavior.

Usually all three of these critical phenomena are present, but any one of them may be absent or imperceptible. The epileptic fit also has the characteristic of being repetitive and paroxysmal. Gibbs, Davis, and Lennox (4) showed that minor brain storms may occur without changes in consciousness or behavior — asymtomatic dysrhythmia. In an epileptic these discharges might be called subclinical epilepsy, but in persons who are without symptoms their significance is not so clear. Among the parents and other relatives of epileptics, and also in the general population, according to Lennox and Gibbs and Gibbs (6), persons with disordered brain waves outnumber persons with epilepsy more than twenty times. Presumably normal persons with paroxysmal discharges may be "carriers" of epilepsy or some related condition. This is one of the most important recent observations, because it shows that a cerebral condition which allows epilepsy to develop easily may be inherited and is much more common than was usually supposed. These observations bring up the question of marriage and genetic prophylaxis. It would be impossible to prevent the marriage of all persons with abnormal electroencephalograms which might indicate a predisposition to epilepsy. There are too many of them. Prevention would also be unwise, because most of these persons would marry mates with normal brain waves and probably would have normal children. When the test is available the physician should insist that every patient with inherited "cerebral dysrhythmia," as Lennox calls it, whether seizures are present or not, should find out if the intended spouse has a normal electroencephalogram. If it is abnormal and of the type encountered in epilepsy the pair should avoid having children.

Inherited epilepsy, then, is recognized either by taking a careful family history or by making electroencephalograms on parents and grandparents of the person examined. By the method of history-taking only a fraction of the truth is discovered; less than one patient in five gives a family history of epilepsy. For social reasons or because of ignorance the facts are hidden. When, however, the electroencephalograph was used to test the parents of 88 patients seen in a neurological clinic, in 90 per cent of the families at least one of the parents had abnormal brain waves (6). A series taken from a surgical clinic probably would show a smaller proportion of abnormal parents, because in many cases seeking surgical help the fits are caused by cerebral lacerations or tumor, conditions which are not inheritable. Probably, however, even in traumatic epilepsy, the inherited factor is important. If a "predisposition" or dysrhythmia is present, the injury or the scar is more likely to cause seizures than if the person's brain waves before the cerebral injury were normal. Of course once the brain is injured the abnormal waves appear, and one cannot be sure whether or not they antedated the injury, although the form, the cortical distribution, and the permanence of the abnormal waves may provide a clue. Probably, also, if the patient has a parent with an abnormal electroencephalogram, his own fits are partly determined by inheritance. This has not been proven, but statistics suggest strongly that this is the fact.

What, then, of the old division of epilepsy into "symptomatic" and "idiopathic"? Obviously it is inadequate, to say the least. "Symptomatic" cases were those in which a cerebral lesion could be found at autopsy, or in which fits followed conditions such as heart-block or hypoglycemia in which the metabolism of the brain was impaired. All other cases were lumped under "idiopathic." It is now clear that the inherited disease is common and can be recognized by the electroencephalogram if parents are studied as well as patients. In most cases of epilepsy there is probably a precipitating cause during life as well as the inherited predisposition; i.e., the disease is both genogenic and histo- or chemogenic with varying emphasis on the last two factors. When the inherited dysrhythmia is very marked the disease may need no precipitating cause to bring it out.[1] Thus *inherited epilepsy or dysrhythmia* becomes an entity

---

[1] "In the discussion of heredity, my thinking has been influenced and somewhat altered by observations of electroencephalograms of twins, of whom we now have records of seventy-seven. This group included five identical twins, one of whom had chronic epilepsy, the other being normal. In each instance, the epileptic twin had received some injury to the brain but the normal twin had abnormal brain waves. It seems to me that we can say that epilepsy *per se* is

of importance numerically and socially and replaces "idiopathic" epilepsy. Instead of "idiopathic" and "symptomatic," we should now speak of "genetic" and "acquired" epilepsy. In cases in which autopsy shows no lesion, there must be an ultra-microscopic disorder of the cerebral cells, otherwise the electroencephalogram would be normal. The difficulty lies with the chemist who has not yet developed methods refined enough to show the trouble.

It must also be remembered that there are many neurological disorders (inherited and non-inherited) that are frequently accompanied by seizures; for example the heredo-degenerative disease known as Friedreich's ataxia, and its many variations. The patient may be brought to you because he has fits, but although he has an inherited nervous disease he is not strictly a patient suffering from the entity we call "inherited epilepsy" or "dysrhythmia." The great hospitals for epileptics are filled with patients suffering from a variety of degenerative neurological diseases. The colony population has many more relatives with epilepsy than patients encountered in private practice and out-patient clinics, but that does not prove that these patients have inherited epilepsy, it only indicates that they inherit neurological disorders that may be accompanied by fits. Feeble-mindedness is a frequent symptom and some of the diseases are progressive and lead to dementia and death. Many of the patients with simple, inherited epilepsy live long and useful lives in spite of seizures. Only a minority show the dreaded "deterioration" so much talked of in textbooks.

There will, for many years to come, be cases in which the cause of the seizure cannot be diagnosed. Our methods must be improved. There is no need to dissemble by using a long Greek word — "cryptogenic" — to express our ignorance; it is better to make a descriptive diagnosis and to add "cause unknown."

---

not inherited, but only the predisposition to seizures, which probably is synonymous with hereditary dysrhythmia." William G. Lennox — personal communication.

Classification inevitably leads to a study of causation because the only satisfactory classification is etiological. At the present state of knowledge, this is impossible because not enough is known about the fundamental causes. For example, a list may be made (Fig. 22) of the pathological states in which fits commonly occur (column 1) and these may be analyzed to depend on five possible physiological mechanisms (column 2). In this column there is much overlapping because, for example, anoxia from pressure may be a direct cellular "irritant" or when due to a distant cause it may act as a "chemical irritant." So only the broadest lines can be drawn, if an approximation to the reasonable conclusions from the evidence at hand is to be maintained.

The pathological states in the first column of Fig. 22 may be classified (as to the *genesis* of the mechanism that causes the symptom) into *genogenic* (hereditary), *histogenic* (caused by visible lesion) and *chemogenic* (caused by other microscopic structural change). To complete the list one should add *psychogenic*, but this does not appear on the diagram because in epilepsy psychogenesis is not causal, but merely precipitative. If the threshold is already lowered by one of the other three, then some psychological factor may be the final excitant.

In the third column, there is a division into hereditary and acquired (histo- and chemogenic). In the fourth column is the one probable common denominator for all fits: dysrhythmia or abnormal electrical potentials. But even this is not causal because it is merely a measurable disturbance of function that must have a chemical cause.

The important thing to keep in mind now, when one knows so little about etiology, is that from a practical standpoint every case seems to have multiple causes, and therefore must be treated from more than one angle. For example, a patient with a drained and healed abscess of the brain began to have convulsions. Knowing something of her difficult home situation, the physician treated her psychologically and she stopped having convulsions. Not that the therapist did anything to improve

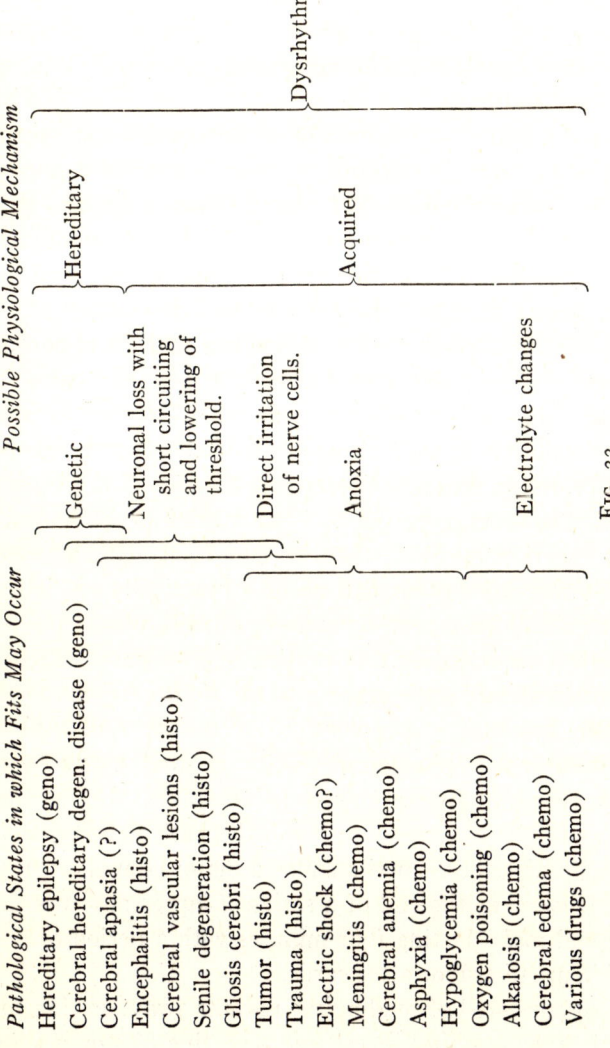

Fig. 22

the cerebral scar, but he decreased the total number of irritating stimuli that reached the patient and thus reduced the fit reaction. Many such cases can be cited (7). In analyzing the cause of the trouble it is rarely a matter of finding *the* cause, it is almost always a matter of finding several causes and giving to each its proper emphasis.

Take for example a young man of seventeen, brought to the hospital stupefied and staggering because of excessive phenobarbital. He was having several minor seizures (lapses with rolling eyes) per day and about once a week a major convulsion. He had suffered from convulsive seizures since infancy and the lapses had begun at about the age of ten. His father was a morose, opinionated person with alcoholism and an abnormal electroencephalogram. He had beaten the boy for "absent-mindedness" when the lapses began at ten. The mother was kind and loyal, but oversolicitous, and watched the boy by inches, never giving him any liberty. At the age of sixteen the boy had tried to rebel, gone out and had a brief alcoholic spree and a sex experience. Since then he had been watched even more closely and his mother had become practically his jailer. The father "would have nothing more to do with him."

Neurological examination and routine history gave evidence of a difficult birth and some trauma to the right cerebral hemisphere. The laboratory examinations were not remarkable, except the electroencephalogram, which showed many large delta waves (Fig. 23) often accompanied by spikes. These came in bursts lasting 5 to 20 seconds when the patient had one of his lapses. Besides these "petits mals" a major convulsion was observed. It came at the end of a series of lapses and was the typical "grand mal," lasting four minutes with a period of one and a half hours of stupor afterwards.

Treatment consisted of sending the parents away, getting the boy over his phenobarbital intoxication, putting him on a good regime with phenobarbital only at ten p.m. Then a year and a half was spent in "socializing" him. He hated all authority at first, but was soon made to feel that he "belonged" and was appreciated. He was given occupation and had a male nurse for six months and weekly interviews with a psychiatrist. Later

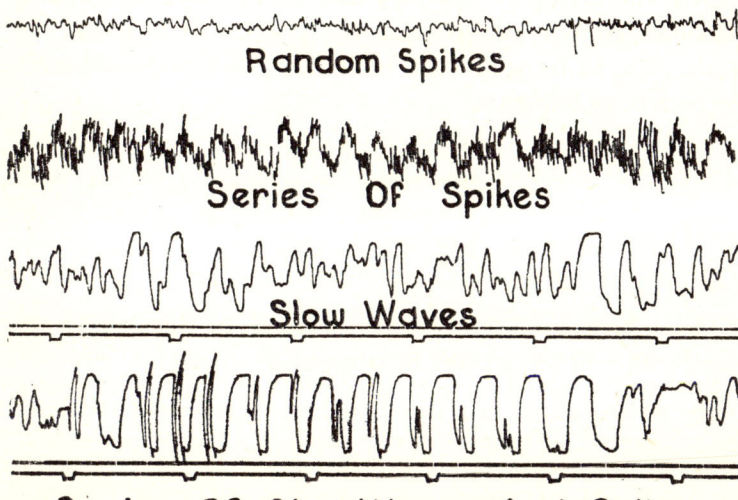

Fig. 23

Electroencephalogram of four types of epileptic discharge. Time shown on bottom line, one second intervals with depression of line at end of every second. The main characteristics of epileptic waves in the electroencephalogram are, *first*, their height (abnormally high voltage), and *secondly*, that they appear in bursts or sequences. There is no good correlation between type of electroencephalogram and type of clinical fit. All kinds of waves may appear in any type of fit. In general, however, one may say that the random spikes (line 1) are common in traumatic epilepsy. The rapid series of large spikes (line 2) are seen often in severe convulsions, but are difficult to distinguish from the muscle potentials caused by muscle spasm. The large slow waves (line 3) are found in various states of impaired consciousness (cf. Fig. 20) from the short lapses of a few seconds, to the long confused periods of psychic fits, peculiar behavior, and figures. The series of alternating slow waves and spikes (line 4) are most usual in the typical short lapses of "petit mal," but may appear in other types of seizure.

he was allowed to run his own life, as long as he reported every two weeks. During the last year he has had no major convulsions and only one or two lapses a week, at irregular intervals. Socially he is a changed human being.

How does one make an etiological classification of such a case? From the data in hand, it seems probable that there is inherited "cerebral dysrhythmia." Birth trauma is a possibility, and the effects of psychotherapy indicate that there was a large emotional element precipitating the attacks. It is nearer the truth, then, to recognize this multiplicity of causes and score the patient as follows:

Probable etiology
Genogenic   ++
Histogenic   +?
Chemogenic   o?
Psychogenic   ++

James Jackson (8), a wise physician of the first half of the nineteenth century, writing in 1855, said:

The exciting causes of epilepsy are better known than the proximate cause; yet we cannot, in every instance, satisfy ourselves as to those. It would seem that any cause, disturbing the body or the mind, in an epileptic subject, may give rise to a paroxysm.

That holds true today. We have found the proximate cause of fits in many cases by the advances in our knowledge of pathology, but in most cases we still have to rely on treating the exciting causes, which may be varied and difficult to discover. Eighty years later at a meeting of the Association for Research in Nervous and Mental Disease, L. Pierce Clark said:

It is not possible to shirk the task of attempting continually to solve the problem of epilepsy. . . . The epileptic and not the disease must be the main concern of therapeutics.

Little as I agree with Clark's (9) concept of the "pre-epileptic character" and his interpretation of the fit as a "flight from reality," I admire his attitude towards the patient and commend it to all physicians. It is obvious that one must attack a symptom such as the epileptic fit from a number of angles and not limit therapy to any one line. Although this may not give data that is easily analyzed by the epileptologist, yet all data on the treatment of human beings is so complex that conclusions cannot be drawn from a small number of cases. Conclusions must of necessity come from wide experience with a large number of similar cases observed over a period of years.

REFERENCES

1. COBB, S.: Electromyographic studies of experimental convulsions. *Brain.* 47:70. 1924.
2. ROSETT, J.: The epileptic seizure. *Arch. Neurol. & Psychiat.* 21:731. 1929.
3. PENFIELD, W., ERICKSON, T. C.: Epilepsy and cerebral localization. C. C. Thomas: Springfield, 1941. 623 p.
4. GIBBS, F. A., DAVIS, H., LENNOX, W. G.: The electro-encephalogram in epilepsy and in conditions of impaired consciousness. *Arch. Neurol. & Psychiat.* 34:1133. 1935.
5. LENNOX, WILLIAM G.: Science and seizures. Paul B. Hoeber, Inc.: New York, 1941.
6. LENNOX, W. G., GIBBS, E. L., GIBBS, F. A.: Inheritance of cerebral dysrhythmia and epilepsy. *Arch. Neurol. & Psychiat.* 44:1155. 1940.
7. COBB, S.: Psychiatric approach to the treatment of epilepsy. *Am. J. Psy.* 96:1009–1021. 1940.
8. JACKSON, JAMES H.: Letters to a young physician just entering upon practice. Phillips, Lampson & Co.: Boston, 1855.
9. CLARK, L. P.: The psychobiologic concept of essential epilepsy. *Res. Pub. Assoc. Res. Nerv. Ment. Dis.* 7:65. 1922.

CHAPTER VIII

PSYCHONEUROSIS

> To the young mind every thing is individual, stands by itself. By and by, it finds how to join two things and see in them one nature; then three, then three thousand; and so, tyrannized over by its own unifying instinct, it goes on tying things together, diminishing anomalies, discovering roots running under ground whereby contrary and remote things cohere and flower out from one stem. It presently learns that since the dawn of history there has been a constant accumulation and classifying of facts. But what is classification but the perceiving that these objects are not chaotic, and are not foreign, but have a law which is also a law of the human mind?
>
> RALPH WALDO EMERSON, *The American Scholar*, 1837.

THIS chapter does not attempt to treat in an orderly way the symptoms, etiology and therapy of the different types of psychoneurosis. For such discussion the reader is referred to special texts (1) (2) (3). Here I try to discuss as simply as possible what sort of phenomena I am talking about when I speak of psychoneurotic reactions in man. Since much of the cause is unknown, classification is still far from satisfactory. What one means cannot be put into a few concise words; that would give a false idea of one's present knowledge. The description has to be discursive because of the nature of the present data on the subject.

Classification and definition may seem like a tedious occupation, unless one realizes the necessity for it and accepts it as an important intellectual discipline. Most modern psychiatrists have revolted against the Kraepelinian school, the systematic diagnoses of Imperial German Psychiatry. But they go too far when they say that no good comes from classification. In fact I believe that no scientific advance can be made unless the scientific method is followed: observations are made, data are carefully accumulated, when adequate they are analyzed to see if any generalizations can be deduced. Without sampling, classifying, and generalization no progress can be made. An "individual as a whole" can be studied *ad infinitum* and the study never can be completed. All one can get is an approximation, a good sampling of the mass of data that accumulates as each life is lived. It is by studying many patients by similar methods that trends, groups, laws, diagnoses, and finally causes are discovered.

If terms could be defined before every meeting of psychiatrists and the definitions adhered to by the speakers and discussers, much waste of time and printing would be avoided. Recently a number of representative physicians answered a questionnaire concerning the "Classification of the Neuroses"; their opinions showed little except that hasty thinking and narrow outlook left confusion worse confounded. I agree with Van Wyck Brooks about questionnaires; the wise man does not give an answer merely because an answer is desired of him. Important questions are usually complex, and neither a smart epigram nor an orderly academic treatise is a satisfactory response. The answer must grow out of a point of view based on experience.

Since so many pitfalls lie in the way of him who would write his opinions in word pictures, however circumspectly, I shall try to explain what I think about neurosis [1] by using a diagram and referring back to the concept of physiological and neurological integration.

In studying the physiology of the nervous system, one starts with the simplest mechanisms. Nerve impulses are conducted along nerves, and if the nerve is cut or obstructed, the function of conduction ceases. Functional loss is complete (Fig. 24 level A). If the spinal cord is cut across, leaving the lumbar enlargement isolated, there is immediate and almost complete

[1] A short and colloquial term for "psychoneurosis."

functional loss in the legs and lower viscera, especially the genito-urinary tract, but after the shock wears off there is a limited return of function, some of it exaggerated because higher levels no longer control the lumbar spinal mechanism. For example, the withdrawal reflex of one leg is exaggerated and may even spread to the opposite side as a crossed extension. Thus, although functional loss is the main effect, there is a certain amount of "release" of exaggerated, abnormal function in Jackson's sense (4) (Fig. 24 level B). At the level of the medulla (Fig. 24 level C) a lesion would cause such important loss of function that the organism could not survive (one might say that there was complete functional loss and the soul was released!) At higher levels loss and release of function are even more equal; a midbrain lesion (Fig. 24 level D) cuts out all cerebral function and leaves a decerebrate mammal with many exaggerated locomotor and postural reflexes.

In the cerebral cortex there are at least three more levels. The simplest level consists of the projection areas (Level E). Here the function is either perception of impulses projected from below over thalamocortical tracts or motor integration, the efferent impulses being projected onto lower centers from the motor and premotor areas. Lesions in the latter cause much functional loss in motor power and skill, but also some release (e.g., spasticity of muscles). Lesions in the sensory receiving stations cause only loss of function.

In the areas marked F (Fig. 24 and see also Chapter III) the learned skills of man are represented, both in perception and performance. Here a man (if he be right handed) has in his left hemisphere a registry of visual, auditory, and tactile "engrams," which allow him to know how to interpret what he sees, hears, and feels. There is *meaning*. The perceived sequences of stimuli may come from simple objects or from condensed symbols, such as spoken and written words, blueprints, or music scores. Lesions in these F areas lead to functional losses, known as aphasia, agnosia, apraxia, etc. Little evidence of release of function is seen.

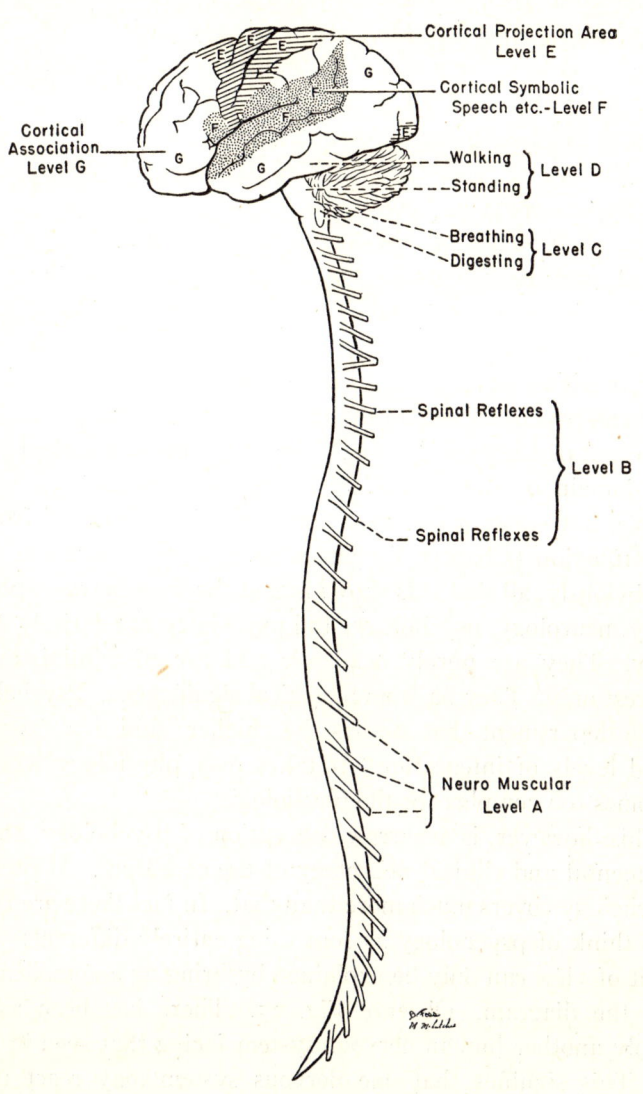

Fig. 24

The white areas in the cortex of Fig. 24 are the "association areas" (G), those that are not specifically mapped out. They are what is left, the mechanism that links each part of E with each other and with all parts of F. Thus injuries here (see Chapter IV) lead to such functional defects as loss of initiative, of retention, of attention. Release is perhaps represented by silly hyperactivity and euphoria.

Any of us would consider the levels A, B, C, and D as physiological and neurological; the people who study them are physiologists and neurologists. Level E is not so clear; many psychologists busy themselves with perception. Level F is the no-man's-land of neuropsychiatry, studied by some neurologists and psychiatrists and shunned by others as too psychological or not psychological enough. Level G would be looked on as the domain of the psychologists and psychiatrists by many people, but some of our most important knowledge of frontal lobe function (Chapter V) has come from neurosurgeons (5).

Obviously, all that this shows is that the lines between physiology, neurology, psychology, and psychiatry are entirely arbitrary. They are purely academic and are of administrative interest only. They have no biological significance. Psychology is the department that studies the "higher" and more complicated levels of integration. It takes over physiology when it becomes too complex for the physiologist.

This, however, is a narrow conception of psychology, an experimental and clinical neurology of the cerebrum. At present psychology covers much more than that. In fact there are those who think of psychology as something entirely different; their point of view can only be explained by bringing a complication into the diagram. Observe Fig. 25. There has been added simply another human nervous system facing that seen in Fig. 24. This signifies that one nervous system may react upon another (note the double arrow from brain to brain). When this occurs, enormous new possibilities are opened. *Interpersonal relations* come into being. The effect of one man upon

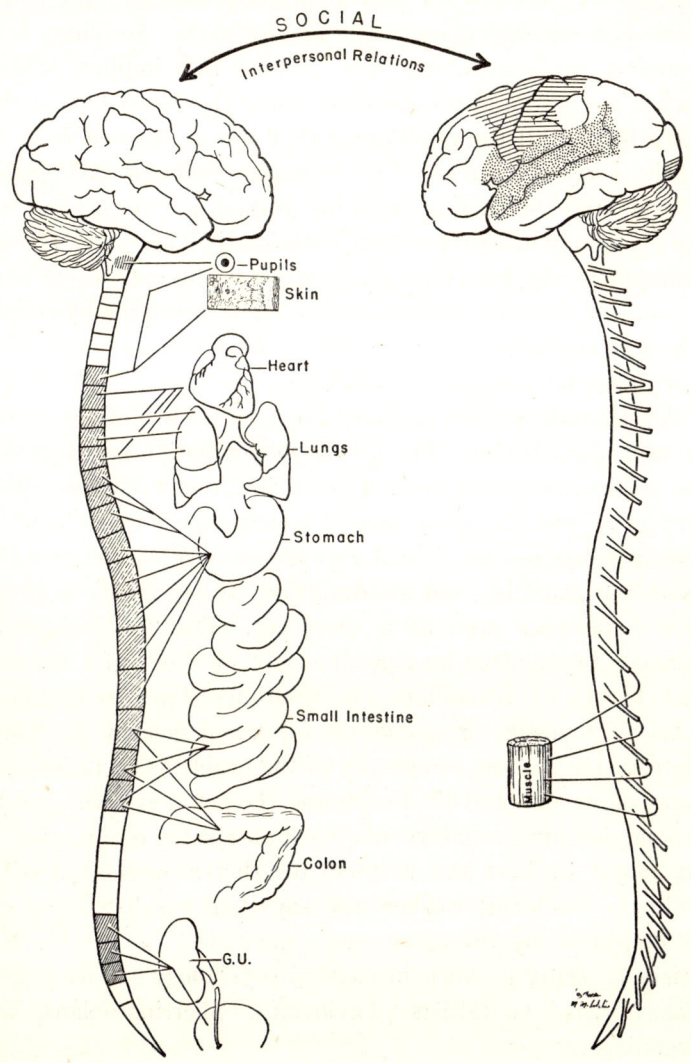

Fig. 25

another may become the object of study, and not only of one man upon one, but upon many, or vice versa. *Sociology* is introduced into psychology, with all that that implies. This is such a great step in the minds of some psychiatrists that they leave behind all the psychology that can be learned from the single nervous system. For example, Sullivan (6) defines "Psychiatry" on each issue of his journal as "the Biology and the Pathology of Interpersonal Relations." This is just another example of the fact that academic divisions and these short definitions are inaccurate epigrams, merely showing what some editor or administrator is interested in, what his emphasis is. They have no biological significance.

A multitude of observations have been made on the behavior of man towards man. The greatest contribution is still that of the inspired poets and prose writers; intuition still plays a great part even with the most careful psychological investigator of human relationships. Social experiments are so complex that short cuts must be used and intuition (to my mind) is simply wide experience used as a short cut. The "psychologically minded" psychiatrist may get the right "feeling" of a situation and make an immediate contribution. The "scientifically minded" investigator makes up for the deficiency in control material and for the complexity of the problems by insisting on many cases and statistical evidence. To get ahead with the job of studying human nature, one must accept the observations of all honest workers and fit them together as well as possible. Only the intolerant worker who says that results "never can be obtained" by the other man's methods is to be ridiculed. There is plenty of work in medical psychology for more good Behaviorists, Gestaltists, Pavlovians, Sherringtonians, and Freudians.

One generalization that seems to come out from the clinical data related to Fig. 25 is that when one nervous system plays upon another in an abnormal way (when, as the social worker says, "there is maladjustment") this is expressed in the responsive person largely through the *autonomic* nervous system, and largely by *increase* of function. Functional loss and some neurological release were the characteristics of neurological lesions shown in the isolated nervous system in Fig. 24. Stimulation and overreaction seem to be the main result when man plays upon man. Feeling is an important element, giving duration and continuity to the reactions. In short, *emotions* are expressed in an exaggerated way by the blood vessels of the skin (blushing and paling), by the heart rate (stopping and palpitating), by sighing or panting, by sweating and urinating. They are even expressed by vomiting and defecating in the more severe situations.

Although emotional maladjustments are conspicuously expressed by way of the autonomic nervous system, the cerebrospinal system and striated muscles must not be overlooked. Occasionally most of the symptoms in a neurotic patient are in this system, muscular tension and tremor being clinically obvious.

Jacobson (7) has shown that such tension of striated muscle is a common symptom of nervousness, anxiety neurosis and the system neuroses (see page 129). In fact he believes that it is the main symptom in these states and he would like to substitute "neuromuscular hypertension complicated by pathological habit formation" for the term "neurotic." He believes that there should be a change from "the figurative and poetic" terms of the psychiatrist to the "more precise and descriptive terms" of the physiologist.

I can only agree that the term "neurosis" is too vague and must be divided into clearly recognizable syndromes to have any clinical or physiological significance. No one is more eager than I to welcome the time when neuroses can be described in physiological (i.e., less complex) terms. I cannot see, however, what advance is made by Jacobson when he throws out half of the clinically recognizable types of neuroses, and then proceeds to describe one symptom as of paramount importance, even naming all neurosis after this one symptom. He suggests that the term "psychogenic" is "no longer warranted in scientific usage."

All this strikes me as hemianopic physiologizing. Jacobson applauds accurate description and precise use of terms, discarding "figurative terms" such as "conflicts" and "escape." He does not see that he is using just as figurative language in his "neuromuscular hypertension complicated by pathological habit formation." Take the word "tension"; precisely used, this means the state of being *stretched*. Jacobson uses it figuratively and poetically to signify a state of nerve and muscle that has nothing to do with stretching, but with an increase in number and strength of the nerve impulses and a *contraction* of muscle fibres. His phrase "pathological habit formation" is worse; I do not see just how he could define it in "precise and descriptive terms" without using psychological metaphors. The whole concept of "habit" is psychological, excepting perhaps the conditioned reflex of Pavlov (another physiologizer, who made a great contribution to psychology, but never would admit that there was such a science as psychology). His conditioned reflexes, however, were almost entirely observed in dogs; some workers have applied them to other animals, and a few observations on man show that similar mechanisms can be elicited in the human nervous system. But the whole idea that habit formation and the learning process are now understood because of Pavlov's work is largely reasoning by unverified analogy. In the honest observation of human behavior, clinical or physiological, one finds just as good evidence for "conflict" and "escape" as for "habit." One cannot arbitrarily simplify the problem to fit "physiological conceptions" when the facts are many and complex. Nevertheless, Jacobson's observations on "neuromuscular tension" are important and give to the psychiatrist a good method for recording an important symptom of nervousness, as well as a point of attack for therapy. In fact we have been using methods somewhat similar to his for some time at the Massachusetts General Hospital and agree with his findings but not his intolerance.

Many other men have tried to classify mental disorders by one criterion. Jacobson is in good company. Watson believed that behavior was everything, overt action, conditioned and unconditioned reflexes added up to make a personality. Kraepelin looked at mental disorders with a prognosticating eye; he classified symptoms in the light of what would happen to the patients who exhibited certain main symptoms and syndromes. Kretschmer correlated body configuration with mental symptomatology. All of these investigations are valid; the investigators, however, are not sound unless they can take other workers' points of view, as well as their own hobby, and admit that the phenomenology of psychiatry is extremely complex and cannot be honestly boiled down to a simple residue by physiologizing, body-typing, or prognosticating.

Psychological Types

Of course most maladjustments to environment are not grossly expressed in tremor, spasm, sweating, etc.; the situation is usually not severe enough to cause obvious vegetative and muscular symptoms. People get into the habit of certain forms of over-reaction to "the slings and arrows of outrageous fortune" and take them as reactions natural for themselves: "That's the way I'm made," is the explanation of most folks to such self-observation. But it is not so simple as that. When one watches people with a behavioristic eye, it soon appears that, although each is unique, the mass can be divided into groups that react somewhat similarly. Psychological types appear.

Typing humanity is an old sport, from Hippocrates, who divided mankind into the *habitus appoplecticus* and the *habitus phthisicus*, through Walker in 1852 with his "Nutritive beauty" (Venus), "Locomotive beauty" (Diana), and "Mental beauty" (Minerva), to Kretschmer in 1925 with his widely accepted "pyknic, athletic, and asthenic" types. All had more or less definite ideas that these body types corresponded to mental traits. Sheldon (8) has taken three aspects of bodily constitution, which he selected after many preliminary observations. These he calls "endomorphy," "mesomorphy," and "ectomorphy," and they appear to behave in morphology "as though each were a component of structure — something which enters in different amounts into the making of a body." They are identified by making standard photographs of three views of the naked subject. Briefly put, endomorphy can be described as the dominant component in the soft, round people with big viscera. Mesomorphy means a predominance of muscle and bone. Ectomorphy describes the lean, fragile type with relatively large skin area and brain. The analogy with the three embryonic layers is obvious. Everybody recognizes the usual psychological concomitants in the extreme cases. The endomorph is the jolly fat man, the mesomorph the burly athlete, and the ectomorph the nervous bookkorm. Thus, the gross body-build seems to go along with psychological types, but there are other classifications that seem to bear no relationship to physique. For example, Jung's (9) division of people into extravert and introvert. At first this seems attractive and apparently fits many personalities, but more careful typing shows that subgroups must be added. For these Jung selected *thinking*, *feeling*, *sensuous*, and *intuitive* as adjectives to modify either extravert or introvert, thus making eight categories. To me these classifications seem too artificial; people as I know them do not seem to fit.

Other psychologists have classified normal persons by using adjectives derived from psychopathology. One is said to be normal but "schizoid," or "paranoid," or "depressive," or "hypomanic." This gives a picture of certain persons, but perhaps is too morbid and smacks of psychiatric smartness by calling names. Freud used "narcissistic," "obsessive," and "hysterical," going out of the realms of normal to take his analogies from the neurotically ill, but his great interest was, of course, in the psychological mechanisms rather than in diagnosis. Murray (10) tries to describe behavior in terms of the inward needs of a person related to the outward press, taking for granted the fundamental, inherited characters of the organism.

At the present stage of our knowledge it seems to me better to be more frankly descriptive because the other classifications are not yet proven to be based on adequate evidence.

The Freudian classification aims at the right goal because it aims at etiology, referring to the psychological mechanism that may be responsible for the type of behavior. But Freud knew that more than one type of mechanism was involved, that all levels of functioning were integrated to make a person. In fact he is known to have said on more than one occasion that "the doctor with the syringe" stands in the background and eventually will make the psychoanalytic treatment of the neuroses unnecessary. This point of view is also mentioned in his writings. In 1928 (11) he wrote: "Because of the essential unity of the two things that we divide into somatic and psychic, one may prophesy that the day will come when the avenue from biology and chemistry to the phenomenon of neurosis will be open for our understanding and we hope also for therapy."

In other words Freud understood that chemical agents could influence feelings and actions, and that emotions could change chemical reactions in the body. He saw through and beyond the dualistic nonsense of "organic or functional." An etiological classification is the eventual goal, but at present psychiatrists are experimenting with and trying out preliminary approximations of what may be the eventual truth. Good clinical descriptions of either normal or abnormal types of reaction are always valid and useful. One of the most recent and best descriptive efforts is that of Sullivan (6). For example in describing the people usually labelled "psychopathic personality" he uses the adjective "fugitive," "disappointing," "disconcerting," and "unreliable." The hysterics are "self-absorbed, fantastic and misinformed," while the schizoids are "sensitive, withdrawn, idealistic, and lonely." This gives some idea of the descriptions, which are long and must be read to be appreciated. The point is, diagnostic terms can be used if well defined in a descriptive way. In fact, one must have such terms, because the descriptions are too unwieldy. Unless one classifies, no advance can be made. Looking on each person as an individual and treating him as such would be endless. Putting one's thoughts and observations in order is a necessary part of scientific procedure.

At present I am using a descriptive classification as follows:

Classification of the Psychoneuroses

	Frequency among patients in M.G.H. psychiatric clinic, 1941 (861 patients)
(Normal)	
Nervousness (exaggerations of physiological reactions)	Less than 1 per cent
Anxiety attacks	27 " "
System reactions (psychosomatic)	18 " "
Depressive reactions	23 " "
Hysteria	5 " "
Obsessive and compulsive reactions	2 " "
Hypochondriasis	Less than 1 " "
Anorexia nervosa	Less than 1 " "
(Schizo-affective psychoses)	

It is freely admitted that many intergradations and combinations of these phenomena are found in clinical experience, yet the groups have validity because a majority of cases seem to fit in, and because other clinics, that understand that these are nothing but descriptive groups, seem to be able to speak our language. Confusion arises where muddled thinking allows etiological criteria to be mixed with descriptive material. I have explained in Chapter I how the etiological factors can be defined and evaluated (page 21). This classification is descriptive.

In the first place one must accept the fact that "normal" is a range of values about the mean of a distribution curve. The average man and those near him are normal, the most "perfect" specimen (if one could imagine such a specimen, and perfect for what?) would be far from normal.

"*Nervousness*" is used to describe that great group of persons, normal from most points of view, who show *exaggerated autonomic and neuro-muscular responses* when under emotional stress. The necessity of standing up and speaking a few words may make them tremble, flush, pant, palpitate, and have a dry mouth. The fear of exhibiting themselves in public may cause polyuria or diarrhoea. Cannon (12) explains such symptoms as a normal reaction to fear and rage. Riggs (13) has shown how education may help persons to overcome symptoms. In spite of these phenomena being almost within the limits of normal, they do seem to occur most often in hypersensitive, anxious people. Thus the line between these and those of the next category cannot be a sharp one.

The *anxiety attack* is a special type of reaction. These patients seem to be well most of the time, but on occasions have attacks in which they have palpitation, panting, choking feelings, apprehension, tremor, and other autonomic symptoms for a period of minutes or even an hour or two. When the attack is over they may have a headache and feel weak, but are otherwise perfectly well. The occasions on which the attacks occur are likely to have psychological significance. In the simpler cases it is as if some stimulus, often unrecognized by the patient, set off a conditioned reflex affecting the cardio-respiratory system especially. Any other system may be affected, but since an anxiety attack is the picture one recognizes as the common expression of fear, and since it is the commonest expression of neurosis in our experience, it is set apart as an entity. Other system reactions with symptoms referable to the skin, gastrointestinal tract, genito-urinary tract, etc., will be taken up under psychosomatic reactions (see Chapter IX).

Depressive reactions are easy to describe but hard to explain. The patients are "blue," "down-hearted," "slowed up," have "no pep," and are easily fatigued. Mild cases work it out by sleeping a great deal and slowly coming back to normal activity and spirits. More severe cases resemble psychoses when they have strong feelings of unreality, lose appetite and weight, sleep poorly, and have many vegetative symptoms.

It is probable that mild depressions can come from maladjustments at the interpersonal level, and such depressions are called "reactive." In fact some grief reactions are like this. But how long should "normal grief" continue? When does it become a neurotic reaction? Moreover, many depressions called "reactive" and "neurotic" turn out to be mild examples of the depressive psychosis, a strongly inherited and probably metabolic disorder.

It is my belief that no diagnostician at the present time can tell from the symptoms of a mild depression whether it is neurotic, reactive, normal, or a mild example of the psychotic depression. Only by prolonged observation and careful study of the patient's background, activities, and personality can a reasonable prognosis and diagnosis be made.

Hysteria is an old term, often loosely applied to any emotional instability, but Lindemann (14) has correctly pointed out that the term should be applied only to a special group, if it is to have any meaning. In civil practice the victims of hysteria are usually women of infantile body and mind. Many of the more obvious cases seem to resemble each other in physique; they may show boyish build, an infantile uterus, and a baby face with wide eyes. It may be that girls of this build are especially vulnerable to certain common environmental stresses, so that they become self-absorbed, think fantastically, and hardly know truth from fiction. They are the helpless "baby-dolls" that attract much masculine attention. Outwardly they may show, in an exaggerated way, the childish reaction of hiding behind symptoms ("I'm sick, so surely you can't blame me"). And they do produce any and every sort of symptom from paralysis to vomiting. Typically the symptoms are disorders of function that resemble neurological or medical syndromes.

In times of great stress, particularly in war, women and men of average physique and without marked psychological deviations can probably be forced into hysterical reactions. Men are less often affected than women, perhaps because they get rid of their dependent reactions earlier in childhood. It is of interest that in war enlisted men have hysteria much more often than officers. After all, the hysterical reaction is usually so simple that it would not be expected among the more sophisticated and responsible men. But it is well not to let a moralizing attitude creep in, because a "tough break" in a hard world may reduce the best of us to this primitive level of reaction in which a symptom is used to avoid a situation, and the procedure promptly forgotten (substitution and amnesia).

The *obsessive and compulsive states* are more at the psychological level than either the anxiety attacks or other system reactions, with their many visceral symptoms, or the hysterical reactions with their "pseudo-neurological" symptoms. Obsessions are repetitive and disturbing thoughts which "come to mind" in spite of the patient's overt desire to suppress them. When they lead to actions they become compulsive behavior. For example a man may be continually bothered by the idea "my hands are dirty, I will infect myself with germs." When he takes to repeated hand-washing, he becomes a compulsive neurotic. A relationship to anxiety states may be seen by suppressing the compulsive acts; this may cause the patient to go into a panic with the symptoms of an anxiety attack. There may be a true genetic relationship between the two disorders, the compulsive ritual being a defense learned to keep off the anxiety attack. On the other hand, fear is behind most neurotic reactions, and its expression as panic probably should not be taken as proof of a genetic relationship between two types of neurosis that differ in other respects.

Hypochondriasis is the state of worry and depression in which the patient believes firmly that he is suffering from some visceral disease. Symptoms occupy most of his thoughts and he talks of little else. Reassurance and authoritative statements that his trouble is mental have no effect. He seeks other opinions and treatments. As in depressive reactions, it is difficult and often impossible to tell hypochondriacal neurosis from early schizoid or affective psychosis.

Anorexia nervosa is the last of the list. It is really more than a neurosis because it resembles agitated depression in some ways, is frequently confused with negativistic schizophrenic states, and often leads to death. Obviously it is far more than a mere nervous loss of appetite, as the Latin translation might suggest. It is, I believe, a disease entity *sui generis*, and was described by Gull (15) over one hundred years ago. Case No. 4 presented in Chapter I is a good example.

The patients are young women who in adolescence become disgusted with fatness or voluptuousness in any form. They diet in order to remain slim and boyish. Menstruation ceases, appetite is lost, but in spite of emaciation they seem to have remarkable energy, insist on activity, and often actually drive themselves to death. The typical home situation is a robust, nagging mother and a passive father. Incipient love affairs or plans for marriage are often the precipitating events. If the patient is taken into a hospital and forcibly fed she can be brought back to a fairly normal nutritive state, but she usually relapses and repeats the cycle after a few months.

This list of neurotic reaction types could be made longer or shorter; as time goes on it will certainly be modified. At present it serves our purposes for diagnosis and discussion in the Psychiatric Service of the Massachusetts General Hospital. As arranged above (page 128) it is in the order of morbid severity. The neuroses with the best prognosis and those most amenable to treatment are at the top of the list; the most malignant and hardest to treat are at the bottom. Having arranged them in this order, it is interesting to note that in general those at the top are mostly made manifest through medical symptoms, system reactions and visceral disorders, while those at the bottom of the list are more psychological in symptomatology. Even though death may threaten a woman with anorexia nervosa, she refuses to admit her weakness and keeps going. Even though the hypochondriac complains continually, he shows little in the way of overt symptoms, much less than the patient with anxiety attacks or the hysterical patient.

Another way of arranging these syndromes is perhaps more illuminating:

HYSTERIA?
DEPRESSION
ANXIETY ATTACKS
SYSTEM REACTIONS
NERVOUSNESS
} (over-reactors)

NORMAL

OBSESSIVE NEUROSIS
COMPULSIVE NEUROSIS
HYPOCHONDRIASIS
ANOREXIA NERVOSA?
} (under-reactors)

Here the "normal" range is put in the center and the neurotic reaction types are placed on either side; the most obviously pathological are placed farther from the normal middle. In this way two groups can be made. Above are those that generally have pathologically increased neuromuscular or neuroglandular activity; both smooth and striated muscle are included. The first three categories are quite easily placed in accordance with the descriptions given above. They are all *"over-reactors,"* especially with their autonomic nervous systems.

Hysteria, when sense organs are often affected, may be expressed by the suppression of a function (e.g., skin anesthesia or loss of vision); but one may look on this as active inhibition. When there is motor difficulty, hyperinnervation is obvious. Thus its correct relationship is not so easily determined.

As far as bodily symptoms go, those below "normal" are *"under-reactors"*: obsessive neurotics are self-contained, meticulous people who do little showing off. Hypochondriacs have few symptoms but are absorbed in anxious self-concern. Patients with anorexia nervosa (like those with hysteria) are difficult to fit into the schema, but from the standpoint of overt symptoms they show little to suggest increased activity of the autonomic nervous system on the physiological level.

The object in making this second arrangement of syndromes is to bring out the point that grouping all these pictures under the one heading "psychoneurosis" (or "neurosis") leads to false conclusions. For example, if one is studying tremor or sweating in neurotics, he would find an abnormal amount if he examined the types above the line, the over-reactors. But if he added to his group an equal number of obsessive and compulsive patients, their reactions would probably be normal or subnormal. The observations might be averaged with the others and the investigator would end, for example, with the false conclusion that "neurotics do not show tremor and hyperhydrosis."

Again, the generalization might be accepted by military examiners that "no neurotics are wanted in the army." If a blanket order were given to keep them all out, many useful men might be excluded. For example, mildly obsessive persons might make excellent technicians in many branches of the service. Ruling out the "nervous" men might take out some of those who give spirit and *élan* to the group. Their quick reactions might be invaluable in scouting or even essential for some types of individual combat. At present there is not enough known about military needs and performance to warrant classification. I merely point out the fallacy of tarring all "neurotics" with one brush. In civil life it is certain that elimination of all neurotic persons would cause inestimable loss to art, science, and the professions.

Neurosis versus Psychosis

The relationship between neurosis and psychosis, the similarities and differences, has been the subject of many discussions and much writing. One school of thought is represented by those who consider the neuroses to be minor psychoses as opposed to the major disorders usually called psychoses. For these psychiatrists it is a question of degree of severity of the illness, a matter of how much the patient is incapacitated. The diagnosis, in a way, becomes social, for a person that has to be sent to a mental hospital is called "psychotic" and the patient who is partly incapacitated but can carry on at home is called "neurotic." This is obviously neither a medical nor scientific point of view.

Adolf Meyer calls the neuroses "merergasias," signifying that they are partial reactions, not that the patient is partly disabled (for a mild attack of a disease which attacks the whole personality, like schizophrenia, could do that) but that he is largely normal and disabled by inadequate functioning of certain relatively normal organs and assets. Under this heading are listed general nervousness, neurasthenia, hypochondriasis, anxiety states, obsessive ruminative tension states, and dissociative-dysmnesic (hysterical) substitution disorders. This nosological point of view largely guided my discussion of classification used above.

The province of psychiatry is that group of human disorders that have predominantly psychological symptomatology. If these were all listed and arranged under an etiological classification, a great service would be done, therapy would become more rational. Unfortunately, our knowledge is nothing like adequate to perform this service at present. The psychiatrist can make a list of disorders (see Fig. 26) found in psychiatry, and even if all the varieties are included the list is not a long one. This list can be divided in various ways. As explained elsewhere (p. 19) the division into "organic" and "functional" is not only meaningless but physiological treason. Dividing them into "neurosis" and "psychosis" on a basis of severity is another useless dichotomy. At present the best one can do is to accept the main syndromes as sound, descriptive entities and give to them etiological explanations wherever these are known or reasonably guessed. In other words, stop worrying over the useless dichotomies. Cast out as unavailing the discussion as to whether this or that disease is physical or mental, psychotic or neurotic and simply make a list of the disorders, diseases, and syndromes we see in the clinic. A great deal is known about *what* psychiatry comprises; little is known of the *why*. A tentative list of syndromes for 1943 might be as shown in Figure 26.

Numbers one to six in the list are often taken as a group; they are supposed to be largely caused by maladjustment of interpersonal relations, with difficulty at the highest psychological levels (Fig. 24, G). These are called "neuroses." Other factors enter in, but the main etiology is probably in the psychological sphere. Thus the group of the neuroses may be used provisionally until more is learned about etiology. Although they resemble each other only in general things like age incidence (youth and young adult), severity (seldom leading to institutionalization), course (chronic but often self-limited), there is little sense in dividing this group off and putting it in opposition to all the other psychiatric reactions, most of which are to be lumped under the term "psychosis."

A contrasting group would be that of the encephalopathies (#18, Fig. 26), where cerebral degeneration with or without neurological signs causes mental symptoms. In these cases interpersonal relationships may play a role in determining the symptoms, but etiologically speaking they are a minor factor. Symptomatically mild cases of encephalopathy may closely resemble neurosis. Only if one takes the several probable causative factors and allots to each its reasonable emphasis does either syndrome come into being as a logical result of various forces. The neuroses may be largely psychogenic, with some genogenic factors, some humoral malfunction (chemogenic), and no discernible histogenic factors. The encephalitic be-

Descriptive Clinical Syndromes
(Tentative List for 1943)   Etiology

	Geno-genic	Histo-genic	Chemo-genic	Psycho-genic
1. Nervousness	+?	o	+?	++
2. Anxiety attacks	+?	o	+?	+++
3. System reactions (psychosomatic reactions of milder type)	+?	?	+	++
4. Hysteria	+?	?	+?	+++
5. Depressive reactions	o?	o	?	++
6. Obsessive and compulsive reactions	?	o	?	+++
7. Psychopathic personality	+?	+?	?	+
8. Alcoholism and other addictions	?	o	++	++
9. Hypochondriasis	?	o	?	+
10. Perversion	?	o	+?	++
11. Anorexia nervosa (and other malignant psychosomatic reactions)	?	?	+	++
12. Schizo-affective psychoses				
a. Schizophrenia	+	?	+?	+?
b. Manic-depressive psychosis	++	?	++?	?
13. Paranoia	?	?	?	+
14. Involutional melancholia	+?	?	++?	+?
15. Senile psychosis (Alzheimer's, etc.)	?	++	+?	?
16. Arteriosclerotic psychosis	+	++	+?	?
17. Special mental syndromes from focal lesions (tumor, trauma, inflammation, degeneration)	?	+++	?	?
18. Degenerative encephalitis with psychosis				
a. Vitamin deficiency	o	+++	+?	?
b. Virus	o	++	+?	?
c. Schilder's, multiple sclerosis, Pick's	+?	++	+?	?
19. Dementia paralytica (syphilis)	o	+++	+?	?
20. Amentia	++	++	?	o
21. Epilepsy	++	+	+?	+?
22. Stammering	++	?	?	++

FIG. 26

A list of the principal nosological entities dealt with by psychiatrists. What is known about their causation is indicated under four subdivisions of etiology. This emphasizes that causes are almost always multiple, and that dichotomizing under such headings as "physical or mental," "organic or functional" is impossible. Thinking etiologically in terms of "either–or" is behind the times. One must at least consider four genetic factors: heredity (genogenic), lesions (histogenic), chemistry (chemogenic), and psychology (psychogenic). As knowledge increases more and stricter categories can be added, using only four is simplifying the problem unduly, but is all one can do now with any degree of accuracy.

havior problem can be described as largely histogenic, with psychogenic determinants, but no known chemogenic and genogenic factors. Yet the symptoms may be much the same (16). In any analysis one comes back to the pluralistic attitude towards causation of the syndromes.

A diagram (Fig. 27) shows the relationship of the main syndromes to hospitalization, ambulatory care, and normal life. The outer space around the outer circle is considered the free world where normal people are at liberty. Inside the large circle but outside the small circle is the space where those mental patients circulate who are under psychiatric care but ambulatory, living at home and coming to clinics and physicians' offices. The two circles are made eccentric, so that it is a short way from the free world to the mental hospital in some cases (see the short arrow for schizophrenia) and a long way in others (e.g., the long arrow for hysteria). Some mental disorders such as anxiety attacks never lead to commitment to mental hospitals. In general, what people mean when they compare neurosis with psychosis is that in this diagram neurosis has a long arrow and psychosis a short one. It is really an unimportant distinction except for executive purposes.

The main point to be emphasized is that the severity of the symptoms has nothing to do with the diagnosis. A reactive depression may be very severe and incapacitating in its symptoms, and yet the patient may be much farther from commitment to the mental hospital than one with mild depressive symptoms and inherited manic-depressive disease. One of the commonest difficulties in psychiatric diagnosis is the differentiation of mixed anxiety, compulsive, and hypochondriacal states from the mild or early symptoms of schizophrenia. Often the differential diagnosis is impossible. One has to wait for years to know the answer. This is not evidence, however, that patients can change from "neurotics" to "psychotics," from anxious obsessionals to schizophrenics. Such transitions apparently are often made, but I believe they are only apparent. If one knew

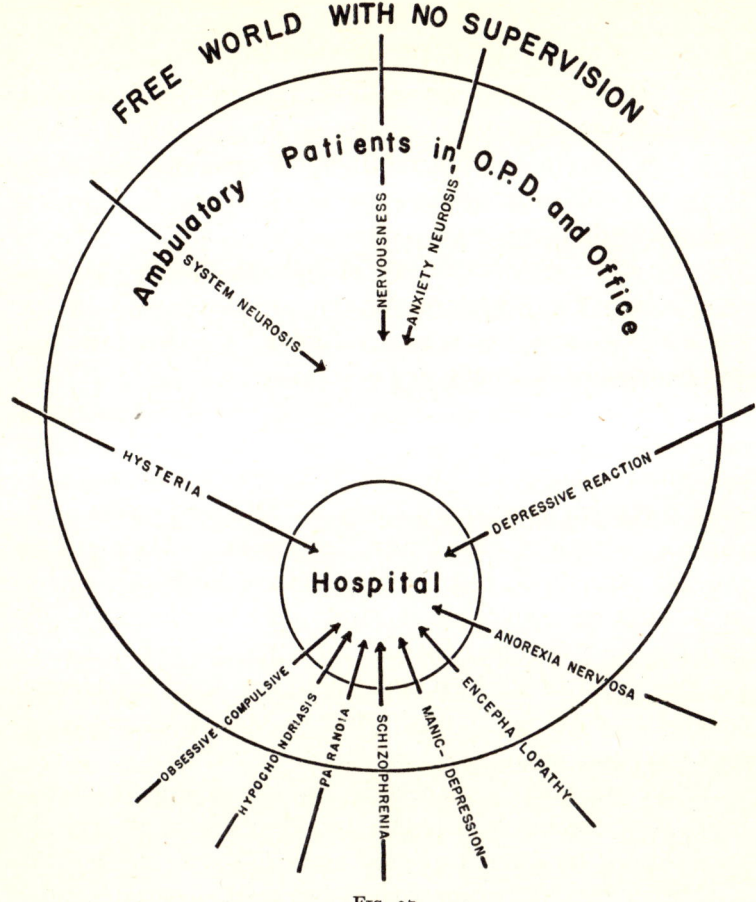

Fig. 27

Certain psychiatric diagnostic entities (both "neurotic" and "psychotic") are represented as arrows partly in the "free world," partly "ambulatory," and some ending up in mental "hospitals." The long arrows of "nervousness" and "anxiety neurosis" never reach the hospital; the short arrows of "schizophrenia" and "manic-depressive" show what a short way it may be from the free world to commitment. The diagram is primarily made to emphasize the fact that these diagnostic entities are fairly clear-cut, in their typical and developed syndromes, and that they do not change one into another to any great extent. Hysteria does not "turn into" schizophrenia. If it seems to, the probability is that the first diagnosis was wrong, etc., etc. Some clinicians would call most of the "ambulatory" patients "neurotic," whether they fall on the long or the short arrows. I believe this to be fundamentally wrong. A schizophrenic patient is schizophrenic, whether he is in the free world, under ambulatory supervision, or hospitalized. If he is labelled "neurotic" for years before he is hospitalized the diagnosis is at fault. Many mild "psychoses" cannot be distinguished from "neuroses." That is why the division into "psychotic or neurotic" is largely administrative and not scientific.

enough about diagnosis he could differentiate these two early in the disease. The same applies to the recognition of mild stages of the other disorders. It is our ignorance of the fine points of psychiatric diagnosis and our seduction by superficial similarities that supports this theory of transmutation. I believe that the different syndromes are of different etiology. The task of psychiatry is to keep on working at causes, until one can make a satisfactory etiological classification. Then treatment can be planned rationally and effectively.

War Neurosis [2]

Before 1915 neurosis was a disorder respected and studied by some specialists in neuropsychiatry but belittled by most physicians as something "imaginary," or "weak." Their attitude towards neurotic ills often smacked of the moralistic; the patient "ought to snap out of it" if he "only had the guts." The patients, too, sometimes felt that their troubles were not medical, but moral or spiritual, and kept away from psychiatrists because they did not want to admit to themselves and others that there was anything wrong with their "minds."

All this was greatly changed by the war experience. Severe neurotic symptoms soon began to appear among officers and men. At first they were explained as "shell shock," the implication being that there was concussion of the central nervous system. This explanation was found to be wrong except in a small number of cases. Those that were recognized to be psychogenic amounted to from 3 to 9 per cent of all casualties. In the American Expeditionary Force the total was about 33,000. In England, in 1921, pensions were being given to 65,000 veterans for psychogenic disorders (exclusive of some 32,000 cardiac neuroses).

All this has greatly altered the attitude of the medical profession towards neurosis. In the first place these symptoms

---

[2] This section is an abbreviation of a review in the *Archives of Internal Medicine*, December 1941, vol. 68, p. 1232. For references, see this paper.

often appeared in men who were considered brave and strong; excellent officers were often affected. The moralistic attitude was manifestly nonsensical. As time went on the psychological mechanisms concerned in some cases became obvious to a large number of medical officers. They had the personal experience of seeing how emotional stress could precipitate stupors, tremors, blindness, deafness, paralyses, fits, fugues, and symptoms of the cardiac, respiratory, gastrointestinal and genitourinary systems. This experience caused a remarkable advance in psychiatry during the years following the war. Now another war is on, and the same problem is cropping up in new and old forms.

Etiology. Heredity probably plays a part only in that some men are born with more sensitive nervous systems than others. If the strain imposed on the soldier is severe enough, an average sound person can break. The earlier existence of neurotic symptoms in civil life predisposes to their reappearance under stress of war, and a lesser stress may well throw predisposed soldiers into neurotic reactions, less than would be necessary to break a sounder man. Of course, because of past experiences and individual conditioning, what is strain to one man is not strain to another, or at least in the same degree. The main common denominator is the internal conflict of the soldier between the instinct of self-preservation and the social urge to "carry on": fear *versus* duty. Other common conflicts are with discipline, dirt, and killing. In some individuals with much "repressed aggression," killing may lead to great anxiety and complete invalidism. It seems that their whole carefully built up education against cruelty broke down and gave them insight into what cruelties they might perform if let loose. This they recognize as entirely incompatible with the personal integration they have achieved, and the conflict becomes unbearable.

Fatigue, poor diet, sleeplessness, and illness may all lead to a state of exhaustion that predisposes to psychogenic troubles. The main sources of strain are danger of death, guilt over killing, responsibility, separation from family, and sexual deprivation. It has been found that the type of man most likely to break down is the unsociable fellow who is self-centered and overconscientious.

Clinical Picture. This is too complex and varied to describe in brief. Almost any symptom may appear. The commonest categories are the rather simple conversion hysterias (found mostly among enlisted men) and the difficult anxiety states (found more often among officers). Here should be mentioned the "effort syndrome" ("soldiers' heart," "neurocirculatory asthenia," "D.A.H."); it seems probable that these four terms are synonyms for "anxiety neurosis," so the total psychoneurotic casualties of the British and American armies in the last war ought probably to be increased by some 20,000 or 30,000 officially classed as "cardiovascular." In the light of our present knowledge these are probably disorders of the autonomic nervous system expressed by fatigability, breathlessness, palpitation, precordial pain, dizziness, blurred vision, sweating, and vasomotor disturbances.

The prodromal signs are important. Men likely to break down can often be recognized beforehand by complaints of fatigue, increased use of alcohol and tobacco, irritability, unsociability, dullness, crying spells, and sweating.

The new things in this war seem to be the greater number of cases in which mental confusion and stupor form the center of the clinical picture. Some of these, especially those seen after Dunkirk, showed extreme exhaustion and tension; they had tremor and such tense muscles in limbs and face that they were sometimes thought to have paralysis agitans. A great number of psychosomatic syndromes are also being recognized. This is probably not a new situation, but a new point of view that admits the possibility of psychological causes behind gastrointestinal, genito-urinary, skin, intestinal, and cardiac symptoms. Gastric ulcer is a great problem at present.

Prevention. It is, of course, important to prevent the nerv-ously unfit from entering the armed forces, probably even more important in the navy than in the army. This can only be done by proper examination of recruits by men who know how to elicit and evaluate a history of neurosis. It is also important to have the draft board examiners realize that the government is now paying pensions to thousands of psychoneurotics who should never have been let into the army. The attitude is too common that a man who is willing to tell of nervous symptoms is malingering and the army "will do him good." The fact is that he will do the army no good, and even if he is malingering, the army certainly does not want him.

In the routine of army life it is important to have proper periods for rest and recreation. Of course war is the most stressful phenomenon known, and this cannot be modified, but, whenever possible, periods of tension should be shortened. Also, recreation should be such as to give the men satisfaction; amusements are not enough and often lead to disgust and depression. All this is in the sphere of the morale officer. The medical officer, however, may perform an important prophylactic function by talking to officers and men on the physiology of fear. One might as well admit frankly that everyone is afraid of death and that the symptoms are universal. It is better to have the men recognize this than to add to their natural fear reaction the worry over symptoms. Many a man has thought he might be going to drop dead of "heart disease" because he had palpitation and many others have mistaken emotional diarrhoea for "cholera morbus."

Treatment. There is great unanimity among the various authors in urging early and adequate treatment. If the patient can be seen by a psychiatrist within thirty-six hours of the onset of severe symptoms, the likelihood of quick recovery is very greatly increased. Full diet and forced fluids are usually important, for many cases of exhaustion and dehydration have been mistaken for severe neurosis. Narcosis is used freely. This is probably necessary in smaller hospitals, but in base hospitals, hydrotherapy should be available. Sometimes the above regime with long hours of sleep, under barbiturates if necessary, will largely clear up the symptoms.

In most cases, however, psychotherapy is also needed. If the patient is in good rapport, he can immediately be given a chance to talk over his fears. If this is not enough, and if explanation does not relieve him, hypnosis or intoxication with amytal, pentothal, or evipal may be necessary to aid the patient to recall and relive the dreadful experiences which are upsetting him. Alcohol or light anesthesia may be used, but the standard technique is the administration of $7\frac{1}{2}$ grains of sodium amytal intravenously. This is given slowly so that the patient at first becomes euphoric and loquacious, perhaps telling of important repressed experiences and often then and there overcoming motor or sensory symptoms. Later he sleeps and may awake relieved. Hypnosis is sometimes useful in early cases with hysterical conversion symptoms.

If these emergency methods do not work immediately, the psychiatrist must begin with more prolonged methods, such as those employed in civil practice. Psychoanalysis is impossible under war conditions, but the knowledge of human reactions attained by a sound psychoanalytic training can be of great use in applying shorter forms of psychotherapy. The important thing is for the patient to have a sympathetic rapport with the physician, so that he can go into the traumatic episode and clear up the amnesias step by step. Reëducation and occupation are important. Back-slapping reassurance, persuasion, and exhortation are as useless as the discarded ordeals of faradic pain too popular in the last war.

SUMMARY

Classification is defended as an important step in scientific advance, because no amount of study of "the individual as a whole" will ever lead anywhere until categories are established and tentative generalization devised. Taking the physiological approach, it is argued that psychological reactions are those that take place in the three highest levels of integration in the nervous system, as shown in the diagrams (Figs. 24 and 25) and that neuroses have to do with maladjustment at these upper levels, especially when interpersonal relationships are considered and social psychology comes into the picture. The systems of organs used to express these maladjustments, as symptoms, are usually those intimately connected with the autonomic nervous system; the symptoms are usually due to increased functional activity.

Many attempts have been made to describe psychological types, but none is as yet acceptable. Even more difficult is a classification of the largely psychogenic disorders, i.e., the psychoneuroses. Nevertheless a tentative list is offered at the clinical, descriptive level. An etiological classification is more desirable but cannot be made in the present state of psychiatric knowledge. Psychosomatic reactions are looked upon as a special type of neurosis, but are considered separately because of the recent expansion of knowledge and interest in the subject.

In writing this chapter I have tried to describe psychoneurosis objectively. Knowing that mere word pictures were confusing and ambiguous, I have used diagrams which smacked of neurologizing, but at least emphasized the large part that interpersonal relations and social maladjustments play in bringing out neurotic reactions. Just here a logical error creeps in — this exposition of the genesis of social relations is not objective and descriptive, it is speculative and etiological. The fact is, one might as well admit that at present so little is known about psychoneurosis that neither the descriptive nor the etiological classification can be used satisfactorily. If one sticks to pure nosological description, such diseases as anorexia nervosa and Simmonds' cachexia may be confused. From a purely symptomatic point of view one could not distinguish some cases of depression from early Addison's disease, nor tell an early multiple sclerosis from hysteria. In short the "descriptive, objective method" sounds honest and reliable, but it simply is not good enough to do the job of diagnosis. Besides viewing the patient and examining him one must go into his past, learn about his childhood, social relations, successes and failures. This throws a great deal of light on the patient; it puts him in a setting; he becomes a person. But how objective is all this? The shortest usable technique would be a social service report plus an interview or two by the psychiatrist with largely intuitive "size-up" of the patient. The longest would be a psychoanalysis. Both are full of personal and professional bias and preconceived notions. To the social worker "maladjustments" discovered in the history may "explain" neurotic symptoms at present; but it is possible that these maladjustments were symptoms of the patient's illness, or were "normal" adjustments under the circumstances. Childhood fears of big and dominating grown-ups doubtless lead to emotional reactions in children; but they are universal experiences and can hardly be used as causes of neurosis. That brings up the question of heredity — are the infants so different at birth that one is affected and the other not affected by similar stimuli? Riggs believed that neurotic patients were born "tender" in contrast to those people who were born "tough" and never became neurotic. I *believe* that there may be much in this, but I don't *know* it, simply because there is no adequate study of this simple and overwhelmingly important point. If there is such inheritance it is probably specific — not just tenderness in general, but special sensitivity of certain organs and systems. On this there is some data — for example, speech defects, as described in Chapter III, or thyroid disorders, as discussed in Chapter IX. How much farther can the medical man go in describing the medical background of neurotic patients in terms, for example, of endocrine balance, autonomic instability, salt metabolism and vitamin deficiency?

The workers on dietary deficiency have described a syndrome in early pellagra that is an almost exact replica of classical neurasthenia, yet it can sometimes be cured in an hour by an injection of nicotinic acid. (16) It is obvious that the description of the symptoms of neurosis is not enough. It is also obvious that our knowledge of social and psychological etiology is only rudimentary, and that we may be describing psychological situations as "causal" that are so common as to be meaningless unless combined with infection, trauma, bad heredity or any of the other kinds of bad luck that may come to a person in this complex world. We psychiatrists are too prone to overlook the simple fact of luck, and too prone to be satisfied with rationalizations of the stories we elicit from patients. We need more data from all sources. Classification is at present confused; at best it is largely descriptive. Good classification in the future will depend upon learning more about etiology. Our ignorance of etiology is well illustrated by Fig. 26, which at least has the virtue of indicating its complexity.

The subject *is* complex. It must be accepted as it is and studied intensively and extensively from many points of view before we can begin to speak with any authority about the causes of psychoneurosis. As to therapy the situation is quite different. It has been adequately proved and accepted by the medical profession that certain symptoms can be removed by persuasion, suggestion, and discussion. (The basic data for this statement are discussed in Chapter IX.) Of course it has been accepted as a fact for centuries that one person can affect another's reactions by these methods. Since illness is one form of human reaction to environmental insult (whether the insult be a bayonet thrust, a billion bacilli, or a bereavement) it is to be expected that psychotherapy would find its place in medicine. The problem is to define reasonable limits. How much can psychotherapy help in largely medical or surgical situations? Which conditions have their pathology largely at the psychological level? Where does the psychiatrist stop and say: These problems are social or moral but not medical?

To answer such questions takes judgment and experience. But the answers of a number of wise physicians are found to be surprisingly varied. What is needed is more facts to go on.

Just now the best data we have are the symptoms found in the various neurotic syndromes. Experience shows that most of these patients have no discoverable medical illness, but have marked disturbances in interpersonal relations which may be uncovered in exploratory interviews. Discussions of these problems often have therapeutic value. Thus in looking ahead one should be optimistic, because even now therapy is effective, and such facts as we have give hope of learning more about etiology.

REFERENCES

1. Ross, T. A.: The common neuroses. W. Wood & Co.: Baltimore, 1937. 266 p.
2. Coon, G. P., Raymond, A. F.: Review of psychoneuroses at Stockbridge. Austen Riggs Foundation: Stockbridge, 1940. 299 p.
3. Mapother and Lewis in Price's Medicine. London, 1938.
4. Jackson, J. H.: Selected writings. Ed. by J. Taylor. Hodder and Stoughton: London, 1931.
5. Freeman, W., Watts, J. W.: Psychosurgery. C. C. Thomas: Springfield, 1942. 337 p.
6. Sullivan, H. S.: Conceptions of modern psychiatry. *Psychiatry*. 3:1. 1940.
7. Jacobson, E.: Physiological conception and treatment of the common "psychoneuroses." *Am. J. Psychiat.* 98:219–226. 1941.
8. Sheldon, W. H.: Varieties of human physique. Harper & Bros.: New York, 1940. 347 p.
9. Jung, C. G.: Psychological types or the psychology of individualism. Harcourt, Brace & Co.: New York, 1923. 654 p.
10. Murray, H. A.: Explorations in personality. Oxford University Press: London, 1938. 761 p.
11. Freud, S.: Gesammelte Schriften. *Int. Psych. Verlag.* XI:362. 1928.
12. Cannon, W. B.: Bodily changes in pain, hunger, fear and rage. D. Appleton and Co.: New York, 1929. 404 p.
13. Riggs, A. F., Richardson, H. K.: Role of personality in psychotherapeutics. *Annals of Int. Med.* 10:13–24. 1936.
14. Lindemann, E.: Hysteria as a problem in a general hospital. *Med. Cl. of N. Am.* 1938.
15. Gull, W. W.: Anorexia nervosa. *Lancet.* I:516. 1888.
16. The role of Nutritional Deficiency in Nervous and Mental Disease. *Res. Pub. Assoc. Res. Nerv. and Ment. Dis.* XXII. Williams & Wilkins: Baltimore. 1943.

CHAPTER IX

PSYCHOSOMATICS

No solemn sanctimonious face I pull nor think
I'm pious when I'm only bilious.
    THOMAS HOOD (1798–1845), "Ode to Rae Wilson."

A NEW WORD has come into medicine. It is quite the rage. One must know about "psychosomatics" to be up with the times. But the conditions described are not new and even their psychogenic aspect has been known for centuries in some instances. What has caused the great increase in interest? In the first place, many medical officers in the last war saw before their own eyes the dramatic development of psychogenic symptoms so clearly that they were convinced of the relationship between psychological stimulus and medical symptom. Secondly, the investigations of such men as Cannon and Pavlov have made physicians realize that the physiology of the emotions is a proper field for study.

A definition of psychosomatic reactions in words is difficult because many quibbles arise as to exact meanings. It is better to show what is meant by examples:

A woman comes into the Massachusetts Eye and Ear Infirmary with glaucoma. She mentions that her eyes are worse when she is worried, so the social worker and psychiatrist take up the case and find that there is a very close temporal relationship between emotional stress at home and the rise of intra-ocular tension. (See case report and life chart, Fig. 28.) No one can say from one case that such temporal relationships are proof that emotion *causes* a rise in intra-ocular pressure, but when other such cases are known to be common (1) and a physiological mechanism based on autonomic control of circulation is known (2), the causal relationship seems at least plausible.

CASE VI

NAME: The Woman Who Was Going Blind
HEREDITY: History of Tuberculosis
SIBLINGS:

HOSPITAL # 48052

DATE: Oct. 19, 1939

YEAR	MEDICAL DATA	ILLNESS	SOCIAL DATA	AGE
1870			Born	0
1880				10
1890			Married	20
1900			Both worked. Son born.	30
1910	Menopause		Son dull at school	40
1915	Pain in eyes		"Couldn't manage son"	45
1916			Son "lies all the time"	46
1918				48
1920				50
1922				52
1924				54
1926				56
1928			Son married drug addict. To Chicago	58
1929	Spots in front of eyes		Son sends for money, comes home. Son drug addict.	59
1930			Daughter-in-law arrested.	60
1931			Son out all night, stupified all day.	61
1932			Son had two "cures"	62
1933	"Eyes paralyzed."		Financial worries.	63
1934			Son sent to prison farm.	64
1935			Lost home. Son in jail.	65
1936				66
1937	M.G.H. "Glaucoma."		"Worry makes it worse."	67
1938	Pressure 22 O.S. Pressure 58 O.S.		Son arrested again.	68
1939	Pressure 19 O.S.		Son sent to state farm, eased up at home	69
1940	Pressure 20 O.S. Pressure 36 O.S.			70
1941	Pressure 30 O.S.			71

FIG. 28

The woman who was going blind. #48052

A 65-year old Scandinavian woman from Portsmouth, New Hampshire, was admitted to the Out Patient on May 12, 1937, complaining of a "veil in front of my eyes and black spots." She also says that her "eyes water excessively at night" and she feels as if her eyes were "full of sand." Examinations show normal visual fields and blind spots, visual acuity, O.D. 20/70, O.S. 20/50. Return for further examinations and for general medical examination.

June 14, 1937. *Complaint:* "Nervousness." *Present Illness.* Patient has a worry concerning her only son. She has often felt as if she were fluttering and she sleeps poorly. For two or three years, she has noticed dyspnea and palpitations after climbing one flight of stairs. No pain over the heart except for slight ache below left breast. Slight swelling of ankles last summer noticed in morning. Nervous cough — non-productive. No hemoptysis. *Family history.* Father had tuberculosis of throat and died of it. One brother died from pulmonary tuberculosis. One sister also had pulmonary tuberculosis. *Marital:* Married for thirty-five years. Husband living and well. One child "living and well" (not true, see social data). No miscarriages. *Occupation:* House-wife. *Habits.* No tobacco, alcohol. Nine or more cups of tea per day. *Physical examination* reveals a well nourished and well developed adult female appearing about her stated age of 65. Head, ears, nose, pharynx essentially normal. She appears to stare. Both pupils pinpoint, slightly irregular and fixed. Upper artificial dentures present. Thyroid shows slight soft nodular enlargement. Thorax negative. Accessory nipple on left. Heart — slight enlargement; rhythm regular; rate 80; blood pressure 190/85. Abdomen normal. Deep reflexes equal but very hypoactive. Varix on right knee. Medium tremor of hands on extension. Rectal and pelvic not done. Temperature 97.4; weight, 134. Urine normal. (Thyrotoxicosis was later ruled out by B.M.R.) Final diagnosis July 1937 was: essential hypertension, presbyopia and chronic glaucoma.

For the next four years she came irregularly to the Out Patient and was treated with an appropriate collyrium. There were marked fluctuations in her visual acuity and intraocular pressure. (Acuity was further complicated by the development of cataracts. The pressure ran as follows: April 1938: O.D. 24, O.S. 22. July 1938: O.D. 21, O.S. 58. June 1939: O.D. 19, O.S. 19. Jan. 1940: O.D. 30, O.S. 20. Oct. 1940: O.D. 30, O.S. 36. Jan. 1941: O.D. 28, O.S. 30. At last she told the social worker that she knew she "was worse when she was worried" and the psychiatric consultation was arranged, which brought out the facts shown on the life chart.

An abstract of a routine history is given above to be contrasted with the life chart on the opposite page. Although the doctor and social worker both found a psychogenic factor in the etiology and mentioned it, the close relationship between symptoms and worry was not brought out until a "life chart" was made by the psychiatric consultant. The chronological coincidence is obvious.

Most of the medical disorders commonly included in the psychosomatic group have obvious autonomic and vasomotor relationships. One can mention Raynaud's disease, asthma, peptic ulcer, mucous colitis, rheumatoid arthritis, neurodermatitis, and neurocirculatory asthenia. The clinician is often convinced by suggestive evidence and circumstantial proof. He knows of cases where gastric ulcer and hemorrhage followed emotional stress; he has seen asthma, Raynaud's disease, and angina pectoris profoundly affected by emotion, and menstruation promoted and inhibited. The case material is convincing, but direct observation of the steps involved in the transformation from nerve impulse to chemical change, to tissue change, to lesion has been satisfactorily made in only a few instances.

The Evidence for Psychogenic Lesions

At a meeting of the German dermatological association in 1907, Kreibich (3) reported that he had been able to cause a blister to appear on the skin by hypnosis; in 1908 two more dermatologists corroborated this observation and gave evidence, with reliable witnesses, that seems to constitute proof. In 1927 Schindler (4) took up the subject again and reported petechial hemorrhages and blisters in the skin caused by hypnotic suggestion. Dunbar (5) reviewed the literature and gave further cases in 1939. This basic fact seems to me to be adequately established. It is basic, because, if accepted, the possibility of the psychogenesis of lesions in many fields of medicine must be taken into account and given careful consideration when the causes of disease are being studied. A phenomenon that can take place on the skin can reasonably be expected to take place in other tissues which are less accessible to observation.

Such, indeed, is the case in the remarkable observation of Wolff (6) and his collaborators on a man with an artificial mouth in the abdominal wall, entering the stomach. In childhood this patient had severely burned his gullet with hot liquid, so severely that it was closed by scar tissue, and in order to feed him the gastrostomy had to be made. Fortunately for Wolff and for science the surgeon made a big one. For forty-seven years this man has fed himself by chewing his food and then spitting it into a funnel in the gastrostomy. Again most fortunately for science, this man fell into the hands of Dr. Wolff, who has spent many months observing the man and his stomach and their reactions to various stimuli. When the man was anxious and resentful there was increased motility and acid secretion; the mucosa became hyperemic and bright red. If these changes in the mucous membrane were continued and severe, small hemorrhages appeared with erosion of the overlying mucosa. In a few instances the protecting layer of mucous was kept away and the acid hypersecretion allowed to act on the eroded areas. Chronic ulcers soon formed. When the hyperemia, hypermotility, and hyperacidity ceased, the ulcers healed rapidly. Thus Wolff has shown a chain of events starting from anxiety and conflict and ending with gastric ulcer. There are certainly other causes of ulcer, but the evidence strongly suggests that this chain of events is a common one.

Situations where lesions result from psychological stress, but less directly, are seen in cardiospasm and hysteria. In the former the cardiac entrance to the stomach is the seat of muscular spasm due to fear in some form. The esophagus above becomes dilated with food and saliva, the wall stretches and the lower esophagus becomes a fusiform pouch with erosions of the mucous membrane. At autopsy the dilated pouch with its eroded walls remains as a conspicuous abnormality, but the spasm of the cardiac ring of muscle has disappeared (7). Similarly, many cases of hysteria have paralysis of a limb and the muscles become atrophied and fibrotic. These changes are secondary but causally connected.

Cases of direct psychogenesis in especially susceptible persons are seen in thyrotoxicosis and Raynaud's disease. Here the dice are loaded against the patients from the beginning; they inherit a tendency to the disease. To use Means' (8) simile, because of the hereditary susceptibility a patient may be like a loaded gun, the psychological stress pulls the trigger, and in forty-eight hours the patient may show all the signs of Graves' (Basedow's) disease: rapid pulse, high metabolic rate, tremor, exophthalmos, and enlarged thyroid gland. This may go on to chronic glandular hypertrophy and myocardial damage.

In the case of Raynaud's disease the evidence for inheritance is not so clear, but patients developing this vasospastic syndrome in all probability have a congenital instability of the vasomotor system. Case 1 (Chapter I) showed ulcerations on her fingers after repeated attacks of arterial spasm that seemed to be causally related to severe emotional disturbances. Yet the tendency to vasospasm was probably latent in this woman, or, to put it another way, her Raynaud's disease was subclinical until she was subjected to environmental pressure in the form of fear and guilt.

Lastly there are the cases of psychogenic lesions which develop on the basis of already diseased organs. The best example is *angina pectoris*. Many sufferers from this disease know that their lives are in the hands of any person who can make them angry (9). Briefly told, they have an inadequate blood supply to the muscles of the heart; strenuous exertion or emotional storm can increase this inadequacy and bring on an attack of angina which may cause death. Similarly, cases are known where emotion seems to have precipitated cerebral hemorrhage, probably by a rapid rise of blood pressure in sclerotic arteries. It is said that every radio broadcast of a prize-fight kills several persons with cardiovascular disease!

THE EVIDENCE FOR PSYCHOGENESIS OF PHYSIOLOGICAL DISTURBANCE

Although the knowledge of the causal relationship between emotional shock and physiological disturbance is as old as clinical medicine, the modern science of psychosomatics may be said to have begun with Cannon's (10) (11) work on the autonomic nervous system. He showed experimentally that rage and fear caused the following physiological changes: deepening of respiration, rapid heart beat, raised blood pressure, vasoconstriction in the gastro-intestinal tract with increased circulation in muscles and brain, depression of processes of alimentation, increased sugar in the blood, increased number of red cells in the blood, increase of adrenal secretion. Pavlov (12) also showed in his latest work the relation between emotional disturbance and conditioned reflexes. These physiological advances made reasonable the mass of clinical data that had been accumulating for years. Most of this was of the "I-know-a-case" variety; experiences, interesting in themselves, but only making significant evidence when reported repeatedly by different observers. There are innumerable patients who appear to develop medical symptoms on a psychogenic basis. In some the psychogenesis seems obvious and causes symptoms in normal persons (e.g., Wolff's case of peptic ulcer); in others, the emotional disturbance appears to be a precipitator or prolongator of a constitutional disorder. For example, the youth in case 2 (Chapter I) who reacted to social pressure by having mucous diarrhoea. These cases are so common that they are "generally accepted" and convince by sheer weight of numbers.

Some cases that have been carefully studied are important because there is much data on a single case. The emotional and chemical changes causing tetany in Case 5 (Chapter I) are quite clear, although no lesion was found that would satisfy a pathologist who sees "pathology" only through a microscope. There were plenty of lesions found in Case 4 when the patient died of inanition and pneumonitis, but the causal relation between the patient's emotional drive to starvation and her death is not clear, step by step, however suggestive the psychological observations. Likewise in Case 3, where unhappiness leads to alcoholism, sloth, and pellagra, the evidence is presumptive at best. The most convincing part of this case is that therapy and social service reversed the process and cured the lesions.

A considerable mass of clinical observation, good and bad, has been published on the subject of how emotions appear to affect the organism. Much of the writing is confused by the authors' failure to separate observation from interpretation, but the observations are so many that even the skeptic must be impressed. Dunbar, in her *Emotions and Bodily Changes* (5), reviews 2251 contributions. Ten years earlier Alkan (7) published his book on *Anatomische Organkrankheiten aus seelische Ursache*, which describes many instances where spasm of a muscle or hypersecretion of a gland do harm to the organism. Like many others in this field, however, the author is too ready to accept coincidence or an intriguing concatenation of circumstances as proof for a theory.

The clinical data of psychosomatic medicine concerns every physiological system of the body. To list some of the most obvious examples: one sees under the respiratory system such disorders as asthma, tetany, and dyspnoea. The cardiovascular system has psychological factors to contend with in such diseases as neurocirculatory asthenia, hypertension, and angina pectoris. In the skeletal-muscular system are rheumatoid arthritis, tremors, and contractures. The alimentary tract probably produces the greatest variety of psychogenic symptoms and syndromes, from simple vomiting, dyspepsia, and "gastritis" through mucous colitis and peptic ulcer to such poorly understood but severe diseases as ulcerative colitis. In the genito-urinary sphere, impotence, dysmenorrhoea, and enuresis head the list. The skin shows many forms of neurodermatitis. Probably many endocrine glands are affected by the emotions as physiological experiments show, but clinically the best evidence is seen in thyrotoxicosis (*Schreckbasedow*) and diabetes mellitus.

This is the sort of material with which psychosomatics has to work. Clearly the problem has to do with the relationship of the highest levels of cerebral integration, through the autonomic and endocrine systems, to the organs affected. I specifically omit the nervous system because a study of the relationship of higher nervous levels to lower, all within the nervous system, would simply be neurology, and psychosomatics obviously cannot take in the whole of neurology. Nor can the effect of emotions upon behavior be called psychosomatics, as in the case of manic activity or of "accident-prone" persons; that is psychiatry. Psychosomatics is by its etymology a liaison field between neurology, psychiatry, and medicine. Its data consist largely of what is known concerning emotions, feelings, autonomic neurology, and related medical symptoms, including the pseudoneurological phenomenon of hysteria.

Granted, "psychosomatics" is an arbitrary term. Accurately speaking, the *soma* is the whole of the body exclusive of the reproductive cells. *Psyche*, as defined by me in Chapter I, is the function of a part of this soma, but the idea of a dichotomy between mind and body has become so ingrained in the thinking of most persons that "psychosomatic" expresses to them what emotions can do to the body, as if the emotions were something apart and supernatural. The conception is intellectually sinful, but at present no better word seems to be forthcoming.

One might call psychosomatics the study of the physiology of the emotions. This would express quite well what most clinicians mean, but would be inaccurate because one is dealing also with abnormal reactions; physiology is the study of normal function. It is, however, almost impossible to say at what point normal function becomes excessive, exaggerated, hyperactive, or pathological. One recognizes the extremes as abnormal, but normal must remain a wide range in the middle of the data.

As well as I can define psychosomatic medicine now, it seems to be a clinical field that takes up the study of the abnormal functions set going by emotional stimulation in any system of the body (except the nervous system) and the study of the lesions caused by such abnormal functioning. Of course one might argue that, since all organs are directly or indirectly (through blood supply and hormones) under nervous control, all physiology has a nervous element and hence may be psychologically affected. This would logically bring all medicine into the fold of psychosomatics. It is better, however, to be practical rather than logical. Just now psychosomatic medicine is holding the limelight because new knowledge in physiology, clinical medicine, and psychiatry has made sense out of the older speculations. Moreover, the war has made the subject one of immediate importance, and the medical officer is coöperating with the psychiatrist to settle their many common problems. It is probably best, therefore, to define psychosomatics simply as that field of clinical medicine where the internist can help the psychiatrist and where the psychiatrist can help the internist in the study and treatment of disease.

Why one System is Affected rather than Another

Many theories have been promulgated to explain why psychological and social situations bring out certain abnormal functions in man. Some psychiatrists believe that the psychological situation, through its symbolic meaning, can center the pathological functioning upon one or another organ, thus causing an "organ neurosis." For example, early fear of drowning is said to predispose one to asthma, great dependence upon the mother for nutrition with over-determined attempts at independence are said to cause peptic ulcer; amenorrhea and anorexia are said to come from fear of oral impregnation. These psychological formulations are very suggestive and at times they seem to explain certain clinical situations in a way little short of magical. Nevertheless, the data from the psychoanalytic school seem to me to present inadequate proof. My current theory is that many, if not most, cases of system reactions (as I prefer to call these psychosomatic syndromes) are determined in their choice of the system attacked, more by inheritance and disease than by psychological factors. In other words, most people inherit certain systemic weaknesses, and these inferior systems are attacked and affected more easily than the stronger systems of a given patient. The man with myopia develops a neurotic photophobia; the man whose ancestors have speech defects develops stammering as a neurosis; the man with a congenitally labile autonomic system shows dysfunction of his viscera when the environment presses him to extremity. Infections and injuries must not be overlooked; a severe pneumonitis or bronchitis may predispose to neurotic dyspnoea; typhoid fever may make the gut sensitive to emotional stimuli. Along all these lines — symbolic, hereditary, infectious — the psychiatrist must gather more and better data before the question is answered. At present one must admit that the reason why one neurotic patient reacts with his gastrointestinal system, another with his cardiac, and another with his skin, is not known.

The problem that confronts us is well posed by Wolff (13), who says:

> If our generation is to make any contribution to this subject, it would seem to me that it is in the direction of stating how much or how little or in what direction these bodily changes occur. If we repeat verbalizations and formulations of this relationship, we add but little. If we actually devise means to study the amount of such changes, we may be able to detect new relations not now known to exist. . . . Our job now, it seems, is to be creative in methods of inducing various emotional states and using at the same time the tools that we have been given to measure accompanying bodily changes. If we do this, we will be able to say to what extent fear is related to ulcers of the stomach, to what extent Raynaud's syndrome is associated with anxiety, to what extent Graves' disease is related to stress.

REFERENCES

1. FRIEDENWALD, J. S.: Pathogenesis of acute glaucoma. *Arch. Ophthal.* 3:560. 1930.
2. HESS, L.: Pathology of acute glaucoma. *Arch. Ophthal.* 26:250. 1941.
3. DOSWALD, D. C., KREIBICH, K.: Zur Frage der post hypnotischen Hauptphänomene. *Monatshefte f. prakt. Dermat.* 43:634–640. 1906.

4. SCHINDLER, R.: Nervensystem und spontane Blutungen. Karger: Berlin, 1927. (Abhandl. a. d. Neurologie, Psychiater, u. ihren Grenzgeb., Heft 42.)
5. DUNBAR, H. F.: Emotions and bodily changes. Col. Univ. Press: New York, 1935. See pp. 373-383.
6. WOLF, S., WOLFF, H. G.: Genesis of peptic ulcer in man. *J.A.M.A.* 120:670. 1942.
7. ALKAN, L.: Anatomische Organkrankheiten aus seelischer Ursache. Hippokrates-Verlag: Stuttgart, 1930.
8. MEANS, J. H.: Thyroid and its diseases. J. B. Lippincott: Philadelphia, 1937.
9. OTTLEY, D.: John Hunter. Vol. I of Works of John Hunter. Ed. by J. F. Palmer. Longman, Rees, Orme, Brown, Green and Longman: London, 1835. See p. 119.
10. CANNON, W. B.: Bodily changes in pain, hunger, fear and rage. D. Appleton & Co.: New York, 1915.
11. CANNON, W. B.: Wisdom of the body. W. W. Norton: New York, 1932.
12. PAVLOV, I. P.: Lectures on conditioned reflexes: conditioned reflexes and psychiatry. International Publishers: New York, 1941.
13. WOLFF, H. G.: *Res. Pub. Assoc. Res. Nerv. and Ment. Dis.* 19:330. 1939. Williams and Wilkins: Baltimore, 1939.

INDEX

INDEX

SUBJECT INDEX

Adrenal secretion, 75, 76
Agitated depression, 62
Agnosia, 41
Alexia, 43
Ambidextrous, 45
Amnesia, 92, 131
Amnesic aphasia, 44
Amusia, 44
Amygdala, 86
Angina pectoris, 154
Anomia, 44
Anorexia nervosa, 11, 14
Arterial spasm, 5
Anxiety, 48
Anxiety attacks, 129
Anxiety feelings, 87
Anorexia nervosa, 132
Anosognosia, 96
Aphasia, 41
Aphonia, 37
Apraxia, 41, 42
Association, 67
Associative functions, 26
Asynergia, 40
Attention, 99, 120
Autonomic nervous system, 73, 74
Autonomic over-reaction, 134

Bilateral frontal lesions, 60
Body scheme, 96
Body types, 126
Brain waves in epilepsy, 106, 113
Broca's area, 43
Bulbar paralysis, 38

Cardiospasm, 153
Causality, 51
    in medicine, 20
Cerebral dominance, 28
Cerebral maps, 25
Chemogenic disorders, 21
Chimpanzee, 24
Choice of organ, 158

Classification, 20, 117
    of neuroses, 128
Coma, 94
Compulsive reactions, 131
Conditioned reflex, 68, 88
Conditioning, 27
Consciousness, 90
    degrees of, 99, 100
"Consciousness," different meanings of, 91
Convulsion, 104
Cortical areas, 57
Cortex, cerebral, 118
    frontal, 54
Cortical association level, 119
Cortical projection level, 119
Cortical symbolic level, 33, 119
Cortico-thalamic fibres, 97
"Crowbar skull," 55
Cruelty, 141

Depressive reactions, 130
Dichotomies, 19
Differential diagnosis, 140
Divine healing, 15
Dog, 24
Dominance, 45
Dreams, 95
Dysarthria, 39
Dysrhythmia, 107, 113

Effort syndrome, 142
Electroencephalogram, 93
Emergency reactions, 76
Emotional expression, 79
Emotions, 72, 80, 123
    center for, 87
Endocrine glands, 75
Epilepsy, 103
    causes of, 110
    definition of, 106
    etiology of, 114
    genetic or acquired, 109
    "idiopathic," 108

Epilepsy (*continued*)
   inherited, 107
   predisposition to, 108
   psychogenesis in, 110
   social treatment of, 112
   "symptomatic," 108
Erectile tissue, 82
Eugnosia, 34
Euphasia, 34
Euphoria, 59, 62, 64, 120
Eupraxia, 34
Evolution, 29
Extravert, 126

Fear, 80, 131, 143
   in stammering, 48
   versus duty, 141
Fear reaction, 76
Feeling, 88, 123
Fits, incidental to neurological disease, 109
   various types of, 103, 105
Frontal areas, unilateral lesions of, 58
Frontal lobes, 56
"Functional and organic," 18

Gastric acidity, 153
Gastric hyperemia, 153
Gastric motility, 153
Gastric ulcer, 152, 153
Genesis of disease, 21
Genito-urinary, 80
Genogenic disorders, 21
Glaucoma, 150
"Grand mal," 105, 112
Graves' disease, 154
Grief, 130

Handedness, 28, 45
   familial distribution of, 50
Hemorrhages, petechial, 152
Hippocampus, 85
Histogenic disorders, 21
Hyperventilation, 17
Hypnosis, 17, 99, 152
Hypochondriasis, 132
Hypomania, 99
Hypothalamic connections, 84
Hypothalamic control, 83
Hypothalamic nuclei, 84
Hypothalamic region, 78

Hypothalamus, 82
   functions of, 84
Hysteria, 17, 130, 133, 153

Incoördination of speech, 40
Indifference, 17
Inferior systems, 158
Inheritance of epilepsy, 107
Inheritance of stammering, 50
Initiative, lack of, 61, 63
Intellectual function, 68
Intellectual response, 27
Intelligence, 27
Interpersonal relations, 120
Introvert, 126

Jacksonian fit, 106
Judgment, 69

Language formation, 43
Leading hemisphere, 28, 32
Levels of integration, 118, Fig. 24
Long-circuiting, 27, 65, 66
Loneliness, 80
Love, 80, 82
Luck, 147

Maladjustment, 122
Mammillary bodies, 86
Manic reaction, 86
Marriage of epileptics, 107
Memory, 56, 59, 65, 68
"Mental and physical," 18
Merergasia, 135
"Mind-body" problem, 19
Motor aphasia, 42
Mucous colitis, 8
Muscle tension, 123
Muscular relaxation, 93, 99

Needs, 127
Nervousness, 129
Neurocirculatory asthenia, 142, 146
Neuritis, 11
Neurosis, 116
   and least resistant system, 51
   moralistic attitude towards, 140
   versus psychosis, 135
Neurotic reaction types, 128, 133
Neurotic symptoms, 15
Normal, definition of, 129

SUBJECT INDEX

Obsessive reactions, 131
Olfactory connections, 86
Olfactory cortex, 85, 86
Olfactory organ, 79
"Organ neurosis," 158
Over-reaction, 123
Over-reactors, 133

Panic, 131
Parasympathetic nervous system, 72
Pellagra, 9, 146
Personality, changes in, 56, 58
    Freudian view of, 127
"Petit mal," 104, 112
Pituitary gland, 76
Postural fits, 105
"Prefrontal lobotomy," 64
Press, 127
Primitive cortex, 78
Pseudobulbar paralysis, 39
Psychiatric syndromes, 136, 137
Psychiatry, complexity of, 125
Psychogenesis of symptoms, 154
Psychogenic, 124
Psychogenic blister, 152
Psychogenic disorders, 21
Psychogenic lesions, 152
Psychological types, 125
Psychology, definition of, 120
    and physiology, 21
Psychoneurosis, 47, 116
    classification of, 128
Psychopathic personality, 127
Psychosis, 135
    versus neurosis, 138
Psychosomatics, 3, 149
    definition of, 157, 158

Rage, 80
    expression of, 85
Rat, 24
Raynaud's disease, 4, Fig. 2, 153, 154
Reactive depressions, 130
Reading difficulty, 45, 50
Reverberating circuits, 95, 98
Rhinencephalon, 78

Scanning speech, 40
Schizophrenia, 138

Scientific method, 117
Seizures, 104, 105
Semantic aphasia, 44
Sensory aphasia, 42
Sham rage, 85, 87
Shrew, 30
Sleep, 92
    and brain waves, 94
Smell, 77, 86
    effect on hypothalamus, 78
    and emotion, 76
Smell-brain, 78
Sociology, 11, 122
Sorrow, 80
Speech, 23, 36
    primitive, 32
Stammering, 45, 47
    in children, 52
Starvation, 11
Stereoscopic vision, 32
Strephosymbolia, 45
Stupor, 142
Stuttering, 46
Subconscious, 92
Substitution, 131
Symbolization, 32
Sympathetic nervous system, 72
Syndromes, psychiatric, 137
System reactions, 129, 156
Systemic weaknesses, 158

Tarsius, 30, 32, 33
Taste, relation to smell, 77
Tender emotions, 82
Tension states, 96
Tetany, 17
Thalamo-cortical tracts, 96
Thalamus, 95, 96, 97, 82
Thymus, 75
Tumors of the brain, 60
Turbinates, 82
Thyrotoxicosis, 153
Training for dominance, 47
Treatment of war neurosis, 144

Unconsciousness, 81
"Unconscious" in psychoanalysis, 91
Ulcerations, 6
Under-reactors, 134

Vasomotor nerves, 6
Visceral language, 77
Vision, 31
Voice, 80
    types of, 48

Wakefulness, 100
Wernicke's area, 42
War neurosis, 140
Word blindness, 42
Word deafness, 42

RC343
C6

NO LONGER THE PROPERTY
OF THE
UNIVERSITY OF R.I. LIBRARY